Please Don't Blame Love
A relationship handbook

Copyright © 2022 Dushka Zapata

All rights reserved

ISBN: 979-8366344814

Cover and illustrations by Dan Roam.

Also by Dushka Zapata

How to be Ferociously Happy
and other essays

Amateur:
An inexpert, inexperienced, unauthoritative, enamored view of life

A Spectacular Catastrophe
and other things I recommend

Your Seat Cushion is a Flotation Device
and other buoyant short stories

Someone Destroyed My Rocket Ship
and other havoc I have witnessed at the office

How to Build a Pillow Fort
and other valuable life lessons

You Belong Everywhere
and other things you'll have to see for yourself

Love Yourself
and other insurgent acts that recast everything

Feelings Are Fickle
and other things I wish someone had told me

How to Draw Your Boundaries
and why no one else can save you

The Love of Your Life Is You:
A Step-By-Step Workbook to Loving Yourself

Demote Yourself
and other ways to show your ego who's boss

For All I Know:
A shebang of checklists for life

Ebook only

How To Write A Book
(or tackle anything you find daunting)

I dedicate this book to love.

Love rocks.

It's this enormous, voluminous, effervescent feeling that blows through me and leaves me breathless. I can't imagine my life without it. It's like heat, like summer, green and filled with color after everything was frozen and grey.

If I feel it for someone who doesn't love me back the problem isn't love but what I am expecting of it. If I can isolate love from all the crap I attach to it, I am left with the biggest gift of all.

Why on earth would I want to rob myself of it?

So, please love. Love as much as you can. Love anyone, regardless of what they feel for you.

And definitely don't blame love for the demands we place upon it.

Contents

Introduction	1
Part 1: Every Relationship Starts With You	5
Chapter 1: Why Be in a Relationship at All? (The Meaning of Life)	7
Chapter 2: Things To Notice (And Do Less Of)	29
Chapter 3: Self-Love and Boundaries (Put Yourself First)	57
Chapter 4: Things To Do More Of	85
Part 2: The Work You and Your Significant Other Do Together	115
Chapter 5: Dating	117
Chapter 6: Commitment and (Maybe) Marriage	159
Chapter 7: Compatibility	223
Chapter 8: Secrets, Lies, Warnings, and Let-Downs	255
Chapter 9: Letting Go	307
Chapter 10: Keeping It Going	331
Author's Note	371
About the Author	373
About the Illustrator	375

Introduction

Relationships determine the quality of our life and yet we stumble around, guided by magical thinking (Soulmates! Happily ever after!) convinced we've found The One only to "mess things up". Again.

We don't even understand what we are doing wrong.

We declare self-love is "selfish", learn about romance via pop culture, and create unhealthy relationships believing we love "unconditionally" when instead we are displaying behavior that is codependent. We wonder if we will ever "get it right". Many of us give up on relationships.

Instead, relationships are a skill. We can learn to love better, recognize ourselves as flawed, accept relationships as imperfect and enriching — our life's most worthwhile work.

In writing this book I focused on tools to become better, happier, better supported, not just by our significant other but all our relationships.

This is what the book is about: learning. Growing. Evolving. Hurting less.

Communication is our glue. Boundaries are the antidote. Self-love is the way. Patience and compassion, in particular towards ourselves, is the only way not just to survive but to grasp that there is no limit to how happy we can be.

How the book works

The book begins by covering what we need to do within ourselves — a practice of self-love, self-compassion, self-awareness, boundaries.

Then, it covers in detail how to grow together, how to stop playing games, how to communicate clearly, how to ask rather than assume, how to set boundaries and how to love.

Love is the meaning of life. It's why we are here.

Part 1

Every Relationship Starts With You

Chapter 1

Why Be in a Relationship at All?
(The Meaning of Life)

Please Don't Blame Love

I was raised in a home with unclear boundaries, not because my parents neglected to set them but because my parents themselves had never heard of such a thing.

In my home, my parents' state (their fights, their arguments, how they were feeling) set the tone for how everyone was feeling. Focusing on them and how they were doing seemed a lot more important to me than thinking about how I was doing.

I was under the impression I needed to mediate to keep things "under control". I felt hyper-attentive, like I was always walking on eggshells. I believed I was responsible for the emotions of others.

My first relationships had no boundaries, because I didn't know what they were or how to set them. *"I love you no matter what"* sounded to me like "true love". My sense of self was in the other. I processed breakups as a total loss of myself.

A lack of boundaries was then reinforced by pop culture. The music I heard and movies I watched encouraged codependent love, rather than healthy love. *"I can't live if living is without you"* sounded total and true, rather than out of whack and clearly detrimental to my sense of sovereignty.

Codependency is insidious and it's pervasive. Spending time alone and learning how to say no are discouraged, put down and regarded as "selfish" — yet these are precisely the antidotes to codependency. It's no wonder we end up exhausted and discouraged, jumping from one needy, suffocating relationship to another, only to conclude love sucks and is not worth the devastation.

Please don't blame love.

Practice. Practice loving yourself. Practice conceiving of yourself as whole. Practice listening to yourself, communicating what you want and respecting what your significant other needs. Witness everything get better. Everything.

What Would You Sacrifice for Love?

It's impossible for me to buy into the notion that loving a lot has to equal sacrifice or self-effacement.

Love is the opposite of diminishment or deterioration. Love neither destroys nor reduces. Any evidence of this is evidence of an absence of love.

Love is edifying. It inspires, illuminates. Love is intended not just to repair or preserve, but to create.

I love the people that I love so much that I want to see their presence in my life transform any future I ever imagined for myself.

Reform me. Elevate me. Come disorder my organized life. Populate it with your characters and your stories and your penchant for vibrant colors.

Show me. Show me how what you bring improves upon anything I could have come up with on my own.

This is what love is meant to do.

Is Being Single Freedom or Loneliness?

Both freedom and loneliness reside inside of me, rather than in a function of my relationship status.

If *"a single person is free"*, this implies *"anyone in a relationship is shackled"*. (False.)

If *"a single person is lonely"*, then *"one cannot be lonely in a relationship"*. (False.)

I can be single and not lonely.

I can be in a relationship and be free.

YES
AND

PEANUT BUTTER

YUM

PEANUT BUTTER & CHOCOLATE

YUM

How Do I Find Someone Who Makes Me Happy?

One of life's biggest misconceptions is the belief that what I need is outside of me. If only I could find that person, then I would finally be happy.

But, alas. I cannot control anything outside of me. I cannot control the world or other people or when I will find this person who will allegedly have all the answers I desperately require.

So I lament what I cannot seem to find. I feel hope dwindling and am convinced that I am stuck. *Where are you? When will I find you so that my life can begin?*

One day, I realize that what I have control over is me and how I decide to experience what happens to me. I realize blame and waiting and feeling hopeless will never get me very far.

I assume full responsibility for me and develop increasing awareness for all the times I am the one who is breaking my heart.

The only person who can make me happy is me, and I don't need to wait. I have been here all along and can start right away in creating the life that I want for myself.

Then, I won't ever overload and eventually doom any relationship with the misplaced burden of someone other than me having to make me happy.

Is Personal Growth a Danger to Your Relationship?

So much of what we believe about relationships is deeply unhealthy.

We are whole and wait for someone to complete us. Only we can make ourselves happy and we delegate this task to another. We feel attraction to people we can fix, we can own, we can "be one" with, and wonder why we fall into relationships that unravel into codependency, disrespect or even abuse.

Relationships are instead a place to evolve. To learn how to be better. To support the very best we can be. A place to learn how to trust ourselves. To grant another a safe place. It's not that I believe you are perfect: it's that I see you for who you are.

Personal growth is the whole point of a relationship.

Can Your Feelings About Your Relationship Change?

Do you know what I want most of all?

I want the ability to put everything into crisp, simple words so it's all easier to understand.

I want straight answers, and things that fit neatly into uniform slots.

Except, they don't.

Life, nature and humans are full of contradictions. The best way to understand anything is to nurture an ability to hold this incongruity.

Not accepting things as they are — messy, in conflict, discrepant — is a form of self-deception.

Feelings change. They are effervescent, mercurial, fickle. When I feel awful, reminding myself that I will soon feel differently has saved me.

Except, feelings guide most of our life decisions. We wait, almost counting on the fact that they will become something else, and they don't.

I can't think of a more unsatisfactory answer than this, and for that I apologize. It's that I'd rather leave you wanting than leave you with something that is less than true.

The truth is that sometimes we don't have the answers.

LIFE CHECKLIST:
- ☐ MAKE ABSOLUTELY SURE mmmm
- ☐ NEVER EVER WONDER wmmm
- ☐ ALWAYS REMEMBER THAT mmm
- ☐ THE ONE THING YOU MUST mmm

It's Normal

Perfection does not exist. As such, it's normal for relationships to not be perfect.

It's normal for me to not be perfect. Happily, this also means I don't need to be perfect to be loved, or to love myself.

It's perfectly normal to be in a healthy, happy relationship with someone I love and sometimes wish I was single. (It's also normal to be a very happy single person and sometimes wish to be in a relationship.)

It's normal — healthy! — to need time away, time with friends and time to myself. *"I need time alone"* is not a form of rejection.

It's normal to disagree, to misunderstand each other and to feel frustration over the fact I cannot seem to communicate. It's normal for us to sometimes not understand each other.

It's normal to fight, most often over the same thing. Fights are not a threat to the relationship. A fight does not have to mean the relationship is over. A fight is just a fight.

It's normal to have no idea what your significant other is thinking or feeling. It's normal to not be a mind reader.

It's normal to make a mistake. Mistakes don't mean you've messed it all up.

It's normal to apologize. It's not a sign of weakness.

It's normal to attempt to set boundaries and to sometimes feel resentful over doing something you didn't really want to do, which means you have to go back and review your boundaries. It's not that you can't get it right. It's that boundaries are a perpetual experiment.

It's normal to wonder. *What am I doing? Is this the right person?*

It's normal to sometimes feel distant, disconnected, even when you've been spending time together.

It's normal and healthy for this person not to be your "everything" and for you to need others: your friends, your family, a pet, yourself. It's normal for you to protect your sovereignty.

In the interest of symmetry, here are a few things that are also normal, but not healthy: the belief that true love means no boundaries, the sense that needing time alone means I don't want to be with you, an inability to say no or express what I want for fear of ruining things, feeling guilty if I see to my own interests, feeling I need to fix or rescue you, placing the relationship at the epicenter of everything so that it feels that without it I have no life, and no reason to live it.

IT'S NORMAL

MONDAY　　　TUESDAY　　　WEDNESDAY

THURSDAY　　　FRIDAY　　　SATURDAY

SUNDAY

What Is a Conscious Relationship?

In a conscious relationship, I'm awake, self-aware, curious and flawed. I am questioning my own thoughts. I am exhibiting self-compassion and have a rich life outside my relationship.

I don't expect perfection from anyone — not from me, not from my partner, not from our story. Expecting perfection is the opposite of accepting life as it is and as such is a form of unconsciousness.

I know what I want. I am clear about my values and what I am looking for, even as I change.

I take responsibility. This was me. It was something I dragged in from a past experience, or something related to an insecurity, or a conclusion I jumped to. I am sorry.

I'm responsible for my emotions. I am not looking for someone to make me happy, take care of me or complete me. I'm not looking for someone to save.

I take time to figure out what I need and express it as clearly as possible.

I am respectful and loving when my partner is upset or uncomfortable rather than diminishing or denying his experience.

I fight well, which includes everything from clear communication to making sure we both feel supported rather than abandoned during and after the fight.

The opposite of a conscious relationship would be the belief that a soulmate is the solution to listlessness; an absence of self-awareness, making approval a priority, blaming others for how I feel, believing that fairy tales are romantic, when real life is where it's at.

Relinquish That Search

There are two beliefs that will guarantee increasing unhappiness.

The first is that someone else can make you whole.

The second is that things are better somewhere else.

This is how you implant a permanent sense of restlessness in your delicate ecosystem.

This is how all you learn how to do is run.

Relinquish every insatiable, desperate search.

Stop running. Let the dust settle. Land here. Cultivate here. Nurture here. Care for here.

Here is where it's at.

Discover this now, or you risk finding out you've lost all the things you didn't realize you already had.

Three Things

In my own relationships I have learned three things that have proven extremely useful to me and that have contributed greatly to my satisfaction and my happiness.

I'm going to share them with you here hoping they do the same for you.

The first thing is to identify what I want and ask for it. Waiting for someone to do something for me, hoping they will just know I want it, is like expecting someone else to read my mind.

Asking for what I want might sound like *"I would love to hear you say you love me." "Can you give me a hug?" "Can we kiss for two minutes?"*

I have found that when people know what I want, I am more likely to get it. This protects me from feeling disappointment or disenchantment.

The second thing I've learned is that people don't love me the way I want them to love me. They love me the way they can.

I cannot force the kind of love I want. I cannot measure their love with measuring tools meant to measure my kind of love. It's entirely possible for someone to never say they love me and for them to love me very much.

Yes, there is a duality here: my ability to be clear on what I want, and my ability to be elastic about what I get. Because, I can exercise clarity, but I can't change you. In order for our love to work, I have to accept (to love!) who and how you love.

It is very beautiful to be loved a thousand different ways instead of just my way.

The third thing I've learned is that I will never know why people do what they do. Asking why they do it is fruitless and keeps me stuck in a powerless, infinite loop.

My rule is that whenever I stand there wondering why someone is doing what they do, I have to figure out how to turn the question back to me.

"Why, why, why does he not tell me he loves me?" becomes *"why did I choose a man who won't say he loves me, when there are plenty of other men who will?"* And *"he will not say he loves me. Is this a dealbreaker, or something I can live with?"*

It's the greatest gift, I think, to exist in that peaceful place where you are loved for exactly what you can give, and for exactly who you are.

Chapter 2

Things To Notice (and Do Less Of)

How Can I Have the Perfect Relationship?

The worst, most judgmental, most unforgiving thing I have ever done to myself is demand "relationship perfection".

I felt for years that I was no good at it, to the point that I often wondered if what I needed to do was give up on relationships altogether.

What's the point? I can't do this. I'm never going to get it right.

After decades of beating myself up I discovered the most obvious thing that was right there all along: I am demanding of myself something that does not exist.

I am flawed and so is everyone else. We get together, as family, or friends, or lovers, and we make mistakes. We hurt ourselves. We hurt each other. We learn. This is how we grow. This is love. This is life.

A Great Filter

I've done many things I'm not proud of.

If I lie about what I've done I in effect lie about who I am.

If I have to lie to get someone to stay, the person they want is somebody else — someone I've fabricated.

If I lie, I have to lie forever, and something somewhere will always be frayed, like a calculation that doesn't quite add up, like a support beam that's rotting and that I decide to use to hold up the ceiling.

I tell the truth. The truth is a great filter. If the person leaves as a result of the truth, what they are looking for was not me.

Now, let me tell you the most important thing. No human on earth ever needs to "forgive me" for anything I've done that precedes them. The only exception to this is me.

How Can I Recognize Egotism?

Egotism sounds something like:

The only person I am interested in is me.

If something does not serve me, if it's not for me, no.

If it's not my struggle, I don't support it.

If it's not my situation, I don't understand it.

I blame rather than take responsibility.

I want to be the center of attention.

Things need to get done my way.

If you don't do what I want you to do, you are being stubborn.

If you don't do things for me you are being selfish.

If something does not make me look good, it did not take place.

I think I'm better.

I think I'm the best.

I think I'm more important.

Any criticism of me is just ignorant.

An absence of praise is envy.

But, back to me.

I am insecure, and need to maintain a certain image so no one discovers I am a fraud.

Ploy

If I were to summarize the most important thing I've ever learned about relationships it's that anything that can be categorized as a ploy is a waste of time.

Which is to say, it doesn't matter who makes the first move or if I play it cool or play hard to get.

If I like someone I don't tell someone and wait for them to tell him. I tell him myself. If I want someone to call I ask for his number and call.

Time is precious and the people I like the most are the most direct and most likely to have the clean, unfaltering trajectory of an arrow.

If they don't like that I am direct and lay all my cards out face up, open, they are not right for me.

Ambivalence

Let me lay out one of the most common relationship patterns I know.

The guy acts interested.

Then, he says he is feeling undecided. He likes me a lot, but he's not ready. Or, there is someone else. Or, you know. He needs to get his shit together.

So, yeah. His actions show interest, but his words express ambivalence.

I choose the actions. I throw out the words.

Put another way, I see what I want to see. I hear what I want to hear.

I actively filter out what he is so clearly spelling out.

I can't blame him — do you see? I am the information selector.

What I conclude is this: clearly, I can make him love me.

Something here feels really good, and with a little time, I can resolve this wavering.

This is the point at which I conflate my ability to make him love me with my worth. This right here is what gets me hooked.

We believe that something about the relationship — I can help you, I can save you, I can get you to see whatever — defines us.

At many points I will stop and wonder what the heck I'm doing. I will hear a clear voice inside me that says *"Pack it up, Dushka. This is like quicksand, and you know it".*

It's not that I don't see the pattern. It's that I feel I don't have the power to stop myself.

This is how I sink months, years into the relationship.

Sometimes, the topography slightly changes. We buy a couch together, or get a pet together, or move in together, or even get married.

Despite appearances that lull me into a false sense of progress, the fundamental thread remains the same.

Me, obsessed with getting this to work. Him, unsure. He doesn't know what he wants and sort of floats along to the current I expend all my energy in creating.

The lesson is this: please, please, please. Ambivalence means no. Ambivalence is unrelated to your worth.

He can be ambivalent about you, and you can still be awesome.

Go to hell, ambivalence.

Wrap things up and nurse your beautiful heart and find yourself. At every turn, give yourself what you deserve: someone as interested in you as you are in them.

Why Do I Long for a Relationship While Rejecting It?

I often feel something at the very same time I feel the exact opposite.

I experience a mad desire to do and not do, want and not want, right and wrong, yes and no, both at the same time.

My stance, my preference, my choices, have a tendency to fluctuate or directly contradict themselves despite the fact I may come across as certain and decisive.

My "solution" to this is to accept, rather than be exasperated, confused or at war with myself.

To learn how to hold this uncomfortable, nonsensical, seemingly contradictory "everything".

This want and not want is more real to me than the delusion I am somehow obligated to feel only one clear, clean thing.

Is Having Fear of Intimacy Bad?

Intimacy involves allowing someone to get very close. It lays you bare. It's incredibly exposing. To me, being afraid of it is the natural reaction, rather than a bad one.

But, life is tricky and twisted and paradoxical because we tend to fear what we want the most.

So there it is, the closeness I crave and need, and to reach it I have to overcome my fear of it. Rather than attempt to tell myself it won't hurt me, I have to accept that it will.

What's it going to be, Dushka?

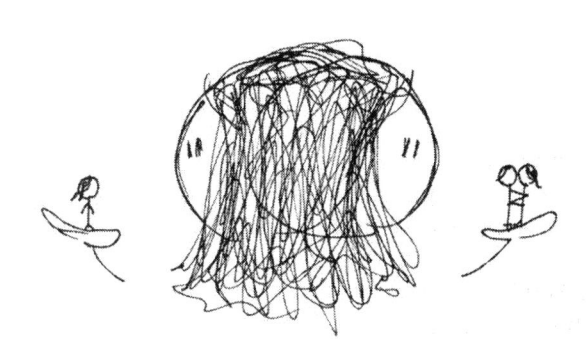

Which Is Better: Assumptions or Questions?

Assumptions come from me — my interpretation. As such, they are a reflection of my experiences, my biases, my prejudice, my stories. They are about me, not about another person, and yet I use them to decode, understand, or jump to conclusions about somebody else.

If I am stopping at my own interpretation, this is an impediment to me getting to know another person. I can't get to know someone else if all I see is me.

It's hard for another person to feel seen or understood if my conclusions all come from me. Every assumption is a missed connection.

Assumptions are an excellent way to live inside the stories I fabricate. Inside this story, I live in the past, instead of taking in new information. I blame, instead of taking responsibility. I create distractions and obstacles that don't exist. I experience anger or stress over things that did not take place.

There is a muscle that gets a workout when I go through the exercise of finding out what I want to know. I ask, and every time I do I get better at communicating. Conversely, assumptions turn making assumptions into a habit.

It's better to ask, to ask so many questions. Even when I think I know. Even when I think I should know. Even when the other person thinks I should know.

It's so much clearer, so much fresher, so much easier out here, outside the stale air of my own recycled stories.

How Do I Stop Self-Sabotaging My Relationship?

Self-sabotage is anything I do that gets in the way of what I want for myself. In the course that is life I become my own obstacle.

Self-sabotage creates a tight, tidy vicious circle: confidence is built by me making promises to myself and keeping them, proving to me that I can be trusted.

Self-sabotage involves me not keeping those promises, resulting in low self-esteem.

The lower my self-esteem, the more I self-sabotage.

Examples of self-sabotage:

I believe all my self-critical thoughts.

I make excuses.

I never set boundaries.

I avoid difficult conversations.

I expect, without spelling out what I'm expecting.

I assume, without asking questions.

I don't trust myself, which means I stop trying.

I never ask for help.

The way out of this vicious circle is to develop a practice of replacing self-sabotaging behavior with constructive behavior: I question my self-critical thoughts, replacing them with supportive, compassionate ones. I stop making excuses, start saying no, hold difficult conversations, get good at communicating what I want, and ask for help.

I cannot "fix" this quickly or all at once, but I can do a bit at a time, a bit at a time, and inch by inch witness the switch-back trajectory of my life straighten itself out, like a clean, unbroken road across the desert.

How Can I Stop Feeling Used?

Feeling used, feeling taken advantage of, feeling like others would never do for me what I do for them are all feelings in disguise. They feel like bitterness, disappointment, anger and resentment towards others, but the person I'm truly upset with is me.

It's me, because I should have said no. I should have said no to giving you my time, my expertise, my energy, and, you know what? Do you know the worst part?

Here is the worst part: It's not just that I didn't say no. It's that I insisted you let me do that for you. You didn't even have to ask.

In an effort to be helpful and useful, I practically beg others to take more of what I have. *Take it! I can help! You need it, and I have it!*

This is how I find myself in the same situation over and over, with different people, in different relationships: you take and I give because I set it up this way.

To stop feeling used, I have to do something really hard: first, I have to stop wantonly offering you my time and my energy. Then, I have to start saying no.

This is hard because it means not recruiting the most powerful tool I have to get others to approve of me.

It means putting myself first: I am so tired. I've had enough. I am finally at a place where I would rather take back my time than use my time to get you to find me valuable.

It's really difficult, but as I slowly stop it with all this offering, as I learn to say no, I set myself free from feeling that all I am is convenient, rather than worthy of love.

Pleasing

To me, pleasing those I love is one of the great joys of life.

The question is this: does pleasing you in any way compromise me? Does it result in self-neglect? Am I, in an effort to please you, disregarding myself?

Don't do that.

Can Past Trauma Ruin a Relationship?

Certainly.

Past trauma can leave me feeling unsafe and unwilling to trust.

It might affect the way I perceive, leading me to interpret things in the worst possible light. This could result in me expecting betrayal or pain at every turn, making it too scary for me to risk getting close to anyone.

It might make me feel like I am a burden, ashamed, or a terrible person undeserving of love.

It might affect the way I relate, making me aggressive, prone to blame, to contempt, to control, to demand, to panic, to shut down, to run.

It might drive me to substance abuse or other forms of addiction as a way to cope.

It might set my filters wrong so that I am attracted to the wrong people; or determined to stay in the wrong relationship for too long. This is what I deserve. This is the best I am going to get. This is what I know, and familiar feels safe, even if it's awful.

I might not know what to do or how to react to stability and kindness because my system identifies these things as foreign and therefore either as dangerous, something to overcome — or something intolerably boring, like living without zip.

I might resort to sabotaging anything that feels healthy because it makes me feel in jeopardy and I'd rather destroy it now than risk losing it later.

I might become a fixer, feeling responsible for the emotions of others to the point my own identity becomes a smudge to wipe away when it becomes detectable.

It might turn me into an adult who does not know how to communicate, who fights to the death, who slams doors, yells, swears, defends, reacts, stonewalls, gaslights, threatens, intimidates, controls, micromanages.

I might develop patterns that hurt me and that I cannot help but repeat over and over — someone please tell me how to make this stop. Maybe I'm meant to be alone.

I might spend all my time and all my energy over-analyzing and reviewing to silence my fear that in the end everyone will leave me.

I might experience an inability to trust myself and my own perception of what happens to me. I become my very own gaslighter.

The first step towards doing what is healthy is self-awareness. We cannot protect ourselves from what we cannot see.

To in turn preserve a healthy relationship we need to get to know ourselves, and learn to love ourselves enough to want what is best for us. To arrive at a place that may be messy but where at least we believe we deserve something good. Because, let me tell you. You do.

What Behaviors Can Slowly Sabotage a Relationship?

Let's say I secretly believe I am not lovable.

I want to protect myself against all the neglect I have felt throughout my life.

In my brain, love is pain.

I want to be loved but when I am loved what it feels like is that I'm in danger.

I might say *"I am so scared I need to keep my heart small"* or even *"this person who claims to love me cannot be trusted"* or *"if they love me clearly there must be something wrong with them".*

This is how I am only attracted to people who are not really emotionally available — people who don't treat me well, people who threaten to leave, people who confirm what I already believe when they tell me I'm worthless and unworthy of love.

If you might leave me at any moment, this is way less risky and way more familiar than you truly loving me.

It's insecurity. Insecurity is the behavior that can sabotage even the possibility of a healthy relationship.

Should You Be Worshiped, Placed on a Pedestal?

I can't think of anything more isolating, more discouraging, or more antagonizing than being worshiped or placed on a pedestal. It would make me feel invisible to know someone is attributing to me characteristics I don't have. I'd feel like I'm not seen for who I actually am.

Perceiving myself as flawed (which I am) grants me the space to perceive others as flawed (which they are).

The belief that everyone is doing the best they can ensures grace, tolerance, understanding; and that I don't operate from a place of suspicion.

The knowledge that we are not here to live up to what anyone thinks of us grants us the space to get to know ourselves.

All these things combined help us accept things as they are.

It's accepting — being aligned with reality — that makes relationships feasible, even enjoyable, rather than impossible, unmanageable, exhausting.

Lost

If you have a tendency to lose yourself in a relationship, when you are single you feel like you are in a state of suspension. Looking. Expectant.

Without a relationship, but also when you've been in one for long enough, you begin to feel purposeless, like you're moving through the motions but something is not quite in its place.

You are not your own priority, because *"that would be selfish."*

You define yourself and estimate your own worth in the function of the role you play — how "helpful" you are, how "useful", how others "can't live without" whatever you do for them. It's hard for you to arrive at the notion that you don't need to "do" anything to be loved.

You can't make decisions without consulting with him, even if this decision does not impact him but has a huge impact on you.

Your significant other is "your everything", your best friend. He is your soulmate. He "completes you". This language is the language of fairy tales, and in real life the language of codependency.

You worry. You feel anxious. This angst means you try to control another's behavior in an attempt to manage your own off the rails emotions. *"Don't come home too late or I can't sleep."*

You need another person to do things for you that you should know how to do for yourself. Calm yourself. Comfort yourself. Understand, listen to and sort through your feelings.

You don't know if that is your opinion or his opinion and you answer questions about what you do and what you like with "we" — never "me".

You can't plan anything without planning with him.

You can't answer simple questions. Who are you? What do you want? What do you like? It's not that the answers are a work in progress. It's that you are drawing a blank.

You stop doing things that are for you or that were once important to you.

You never spend any time with yourself. If you do, you are not with you. You are waiting. You check your phone 386 times. Clearly this indicates how important he is to you.

When choosing between anything and your significant other you choose spending time with your significant other. You believe this is because you love him. I mean, there is nothing you'd rather be doing, so why not?

One day you wake up to realize just how many things you've lost: what happened to the trip you meant to take, the class you were planning to enroll in, the interests you were going to explore? What happened to your friends?

You break up and it doesn't feel like you've lost a person. It feels like you've lost everything.

Chapter 3

Self-Love and Boundaries
(Put Yourself First)

Represent Yourself

If I say I am sorry for something I didn't do, or go along with something I don't agree with, I might temporarily "keep the peace" but I cause myself injury.

I leave myself feeling like I didn't stand up for myself. Like I can't really count on me.

Like nurturing or protecting a relationship comes at the price of failing or even betraying myself.

Over time, this strategy begins to erase me. It comes with a loss of self: I get to the point where I, in fact, do feel responsible for everything I apologize for.

I don't know if it was my fault or not. It probably was.

I become overly accommodating. I avoid conflict, even when, frankly, it's overdue. I go along with what others say. I let others make decisions for me. I don't even remember how to make one.

There I am, obliging, afraid to say no, super focused on the emotions of others.

It's vital that I represent myself. That I have my own perspective. That I let other people know what I need, what I want and what I feel.

I don't need to explain myself. I don't need to say yes just to avoid an argument. and I most definitely do not need to apologize for something I didn't do. Because as much as I want to keep the peace, my connection with myself — proving to me I am someone I can count on — is more important.

Exclusive

I am sexually and romantically exclusive.

What I mean by this is that when I love someone I am not into having sex with anyone other than him.

Even if this was an option available to me, even if my significant other declared he did not consider this one of our relationship agreements and assured me I was "free", I still would not do it.

I am not alarmed by the thought of sleeping with other people. I don't think it's bad. I don't think less (or more) of people who do it.

It's simply not interesting to me.

Along these same lines, if my partner expressed an irrepressible desire to engage in sex with others I would tell him to by all means commence with his romps at his earliest convenience.

I would also instantly put an end to the romantic aspect of our relationship — even before any of this boisterous frolicking began.

Monogamy is (to me) not an opinion. It's not a belief. It's not a value judgment. It's not a choice. It's not a debate. It's not something I need to argue in favor of. It's not a discipline or even a practice.

It's something I am, which means that I can't bend it, even if I wanted to.

It's for this reason that I understand other people may not be like me. It's entirely possible for someone to love me madly and to want to sleep with other people in a way they could not bend.

This would not make him wrong (or immature, or a scoundrel). It does not make me wrong. What it does is make us incompatible.

In my experience, incompatibility is impenetrable. It cannot be resolved, even after ten thousand years of arguing about it with the full force of my undivided attention.

If I am monogamous and "try" to have a relationship with someone who is not, we will not "work it out". It will not be OK because we love each other.

I will end up exhausted, frustrated, tortured and resentful. We will put each other through hell.

I am monogamous, and if you are not, you are not for me.

NOPE.

Self-Compassion

There was a point in my life (OK, many) where I concluded I was doomed. I was just not good at relationships, and never would be.

In therapy I learned I'd never tell a friend *"You're not good at relationships, so you're doomed."* Put in other words, I had an absence of self-compassion and had no idea how to treat myself the way I'd treat someone I loved.

I also learned relationships are messy. That there is no "getting it right". That longevity is not a measure of success. That even the best couples fight, which matters a whole lot less than how they navigate conflict.

I learned that most issues are resolvable and that understanding people (others and myself) is pretty much the most interesting thing I could be doing with my time.

I still rail at myself, but now I see it. Relationships still exasperate me, but now I know to ask for a time out and return when I feel better.

And, I still mess things up but not because I suck. It's because I'm human, and messing up is what we do.

Not Responsible

Believing I am in some way responsible for the emotions of others is one of the main symptoms of codependency.

Other symptoms are a tendency to want to please to my own detriment, an inability to set boundaries, and attempting to control how others behave.

Codependency is incredibly common, even "normal", despite the fact it's not healthy.

To "recover" from codependency, I start by learning how to set boundaries and spend time alone to better understand myself, what I need and what I want.

There is no quick fix. Rather, it's a practice that I observe and keep coming back to.

This practice will change the landscape of my life, how I relate to others, and will help me create relationships that feel safe.

Mistakes I Make When Setting Boundaries

Being clumsy. Setting boundaries that were too rigid or too harsh in an effort to stand up for myself.

Being lenient. Setting boundaries that were too soft or wishy-washy, in an effort to avoid being hurtful.

Seeking approval for my boundary. Usually in the form of setting a boundary and then spending a lot of time and energy explaining why I was doing so. While context can be helpful (and courteous), boundaries don't require an explanation.

Being unclear. Setting boundaries that were confusing or ambiguous.

Confusing boundaries with control. Setting boundaries that were not really boundaries since they were about the behavior of another rather than my own.

Feeling like it was one and done. Setting boundaries, but then neglecting to reinforce them. Boundaries are a practice, rather than a single action.

BOUNDARIES TAKE PRACTICE.

What Do I Do if She Asked for a Break?

I find people difficult to understand. In particular I find them difficult to understand when they want me and they don't, yes and no, stay and go.

This dance makes me feel resentful. How did I unwillingly end up on a roller coaster?

There is one sure way to get me off this involuntary ride: to stop trying to decrypt another person, and instead turn all my decoding powers back to me.

Dushka, what is it that you want? What do you want to expose your heart to? Who do you want to invest time in? Why do you think it's enough for you to be with someone who wants to be alone?

I've concluded I don't like roller coasters, and that it's perfectly fair for me to — as painful as it might be — step away from people who are not sure about me.

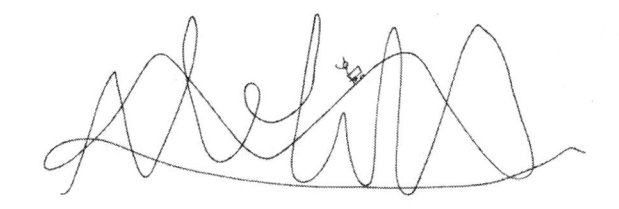

Can Self-Focus Improve Relationships?

Imagine for a moment that I am needy. I need company. I need frequent reassurance. I want texts to be responded to at a certain cadence. I want to hear you say *"I love you"*.

I end up in a relationship with someone emotionally distant. He does not need to see me every day, is not in the habit of looking at his phone, and he already told me he loves me and thinks it's smarmy to say it all the time.

I can focus on him. I can talk to him, tell him I need his attention, explain how what he is failing to do makes me feel.

Or I can focus on myself. I can ask myself how this neediness is making me feel, so desperate and grasping. I can ask myself how it's served me in the past. I can ask myself if this is the person I want to be. I can learn how to evolve out of needing, not for him, but for me.

In my personal experience, focusing on myself is the only thing that has ever improved my relationships.

Why Do I Feel Unloved and Unwanted?

The sense that I am unloved and unwanted feels like something I can't seem to elicit from another but is instead related to how I feel about myself.

If I feel good about myself and you say you love me your words pour over me slow, like honey. They lubricate my skin, bestow on me all their underestimated properties, feel nonperishable, like two thousand years from now they will still coat me, will remain intact, a chemically stable protective cover.

If I don't feel good about myself and you say you love me it will feel like you're speaking out of a tin can, empty, fake, lacking resonance or acoustic substance.

I find that hard to believe, I will say. *I mean, how can you? You don't even know me.*

Or, I will find a tear in everything, misinterpret everything, overanalyze everything, conclude that no thank you. No, thank you. I'm much safer here where whatever you think you feel can't hurt me.

It's not the quality or veracity or weight of your feelings that matter, not their significance or transcendence, but how they land on me, thick and sweet and true or hollow, unsubstantial.

You can love me all you want but on bad days your deepest, most heartfelt words won't mean a thing.

Our brain protects and confirms what we believe. This is why we need to love ourselves. To develop the ability to recognize when someone loves us.

What if I'm Not Sure About My Relationship?

My father was extremely protective of me. In an effort to keep me safe he taught me love was possessive. When I grew up to form my own relationships, if the guy didn't want to own me, it didn't feel like love.

Instead it felt light and untethered, with no grip — like my relationship was insubstantial and could at any moment evaporate.

I bring this up because I had many doubts about my relationships with men who felt I was capable of taking care of myself.

The relationships I doubted the most were the ones that were healthy.

I think it's reductive to say *"always trust your intuition"*.

It's true I come equipped with an inner voice who has a tendency to get things right, and I trust her.

But, I can't call her infallible. Humans never are.

I also come equipped with fear. Fear and insecurity.

And, with a distorted definition of love I picked up when I was a kid.

When I have doubts about a relationship, I remember I have also felt resounding certainty about the wrong people.

So, I pause. I listen to the inner voice expressing misgivings and try to identify which voice is doing the talking.

I pay attention. But I decide which voice gets to dictate what I do next.

This is my inner work. No one outside of me can do this for me.

It's up to you Dshka.

How Can I Recover From My Fear of Abandonment?

When I'm a kid and someone close to me leaves I do not have the emotional sophistication to grasp *"my dad needs to work two jobs to make ends meet"* or *"my parents are leaving each other, not me"* or *"my mom is overwhelmed and cannot be present in the way I need her to be."*

All I know is that someone left me, and that this must mean I don't matter. Clearly there is something wrong with me.

This is the lens through which I process everything.

In relationships, I'm anxious because I know you'll leave as soon as you realize I am not that great. If you really knew me, you couldn't possibly love me.

If I ask someone out on a date and they say no I conclude I am unlovable.

I spend so much time wondering if someone is interested in me that I never stop to wonder if I am interested in them.

My significant other says *"I want to spend Sunday by myself"* and I hear *"I am beginning to lose interest in you."*

Another person's boundaries sound terrifying, unbearable instead of natural.

I remain in relationships that are not healthy because I know no one else will ever love me.

I surround myself with people who use me because them needing me makes it less likely that they will leave.

The antidote to all of this is to learn how to love myself: to show me that this lens I see the world through is distorted and misguiding me and that I am in fact wildly, utterly worth loving.

Can Resentment Ruin a Relationship?

Resentment is poison. It's taking anger, all fire and thorns and bitterness, and swallowing it whole, feeling it lodged in my solar plexus, stuck and smoldering for decades.

It arises from me feeling like the way I'm being treated is not fair and often comes mixed with shame, feeling small, like someone took advantage of the most defenseless, innocent part of me.

Resentment is persistent. I can't stop thinking about something you did, but also I can't address it. It results in strained relationships, tension, feeling like I don't matter and am not being seen.

You hurt me, and you can't even tell.

Because of my inability to articulate and express what happened or what I am feeling, resentment shows up first in an absence of joy. Remember when we used to be light, carefree? Remember when we could hold each other at the epicenter of a world on fire, unscathed?

Then, passive aggressive behavior, keeping score, tit for tat, experiencing outbursts over small things, being cutting when you least expect it. It's making a big deal about how you never fold laundry, when it's not about the laundry. It's having sex less and less, because it might take my brain a while to catch up, but my body is quick and has identified you as an enemy.

In my opinion, resentment is hard to address head on because it's difficult to put into words what is actually happening. You see, I'm not angry at you. I am angry at me, for not being as clear as I should have been, for being unable to say no, for putting myself in a position where I made it OK to be the recipient of what I consider an injustice.

So, no. It's not resentment that ruins a relationship. It's me. I ruin a relationship, and if I want to stop doing so I have to get good at knowing myself, understanding what I need and expressing it as clearly as I can.

Boundaries are the antidote. That, and unconditional, unfaltering self-love.

To Keep a Past Relationship From Affecting My Current Relationship

I get to know myself. What are my patterns? What is it that I end up doing because it's what I know? What are the beliefs that I carry around? Where have I been hurt before? Do I deal with an inability to trust? A belief I will be abandoned or rejected? How can I give me what I need? How can I be the one who makes me feel that I am safe?

I keep an eye on how I am treating myself. Am I listening to my needs? Am I standing up for myself? Do I honor my own feelings? How do I sound when I am talking to myself?

I learn how to regulate my emotions. Can I articulate them? Am I making space for my anger? Am I practicing self-compassion? Do I understand my emotions are mine to manage, rather than someone else's responsibility?

I practice setting boundaries. Am I clear on where I need to set limits? Do I feel overextended or resentful? Is it hard for me to say no? Am I able to respect the boundaries of the people that I love?

I work at improving my ability to communicate. Can I point out hurtful behavior without being critical? Can I be clear without disdain? Can I be direct without being passive-aggressive? Can I be vulnerable?

If I cannot seem to get away from past relationships that hurt me, taking time relationship-free to learn more about myself and process what I've been through is the best thing I can do for me and for any future relationship.

Chapter 4

Things To Do More Of

You Are Loved Because You Are You

It hurt, to finally understand what I am about to tell you.

It hurt, because why the heck had I been trying so hard?

Here it is.

I don't need to do anything to be loved.

I am loved because I am me and this requires neither action nor effort.

I don't have to convince, persuade, chase or win anyone over to get or catch either a good friend or a significant other.

Love — in any iteration — is like gravity. I don't do anything to keep my feet firmly planted on the ground.

These things are so true that if I instead decide to act — to exert effort, to work at it, to charm, to earn, to be useful, to help, to aggressively pursue, to orchestrate — I attract unhealthy relationships and wonder where to cast the blame.

I walk away from any dynamic that requires me to compromise my peace of mind. I do less. A lot less.

I do nothing and witness an upside down life right itself.

Input/Output

I picture everything I do as needing both input and output — power and energy, supplied and produced.

If I go through my day working, running, generating, what is my input, that allows for this energy output?

Am I pausing, resting, playing, sleeping?

If I don't think this way my ability to generate will become first depleted, then compromised.

If I write a lot, what is it that feeds this writing? If all I do is sit behind my computer writing, I will eventually run out of things to write about (or the energy to write them).

I need input — reading, life experiences, a source of inspiration in the walks I take and the people I talk to and the things I do.

In relationships, if I spend every waking hour with the person that I love, where is the input that feeds that, so that the energy I put into my relationship runs fresh and clean and bright?

What about my interests? What about my friends? What about my family?

Life working/life resting. Life writing/life witnessing. Life together. Life apart.

Input/output.

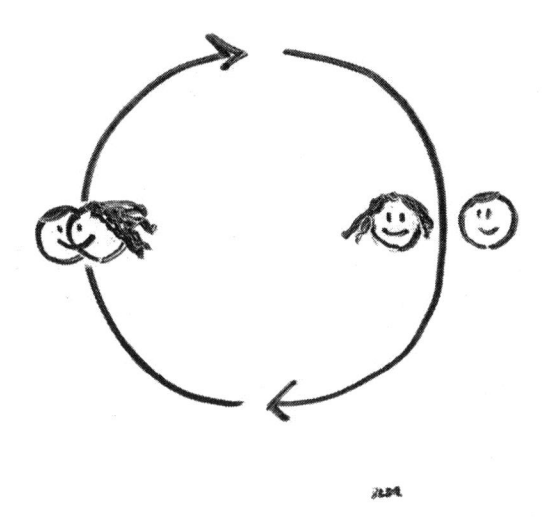

Relationships Are an Inside Job

The things I practice getting in order within myself that have the most impact on my relationships are:

A solid footing so I can trust myself and assume the best in others. This is the opposite of being led by my insecurities.

The knowledge that I am fully responsible for myself: my wants, my needs, my emotions. I make me happy and I manage whatever I am feeling. I own my mistakes and see where I need to do work. This is the opposite of blame, the opposite of attempting to change or control another.

Good communication. An ability to speak up, work through conflict, refrain from criticism; knowing how to ask for what I want. This is the opposite of confusion, misunderstandings, assumptions and guesswork.

Strong boundaries: setting them, enforcing them, respecting the boundaries of another. This is the antidote to resentment and the sense that I have been taken for granted.

A very crisp sense of what I want. This is an assessment of compatibility.

The ability to not take myself too seriously. This is humor, lightheartedness and perspective which is a saving grace in difficult times.

Please note every single one of these things is an inside job — me looking within to improve my relationships.

Me improving my relationship with me is the only way I can ever contribute to improving my relationship with others.

What Do I Do if I Haven't Dated for Decades?

Discard the thought *"I've been out of the game too long and don't know how it's played anymore"*. It doesn't matter how much things have changed, as there is no central authority dictating how things are now. Everything will be smoother if you instead conceive of yourself as the game designer.

Take some time to get to know yourself. If you have a sense of what you like, what previous relationships have taught you, exactly what it is you are afraid of and what it is that you want, you're way ahead of this game you feel so out of.

Date someone you wouldn't normally date. I don't know why we keep doing what we "normally" do long after we've proven that what we normally do is not getting us the results we want.

If you are a woman and believe you should not make the first move, take a moment to think about how this limits you. If you wait for others to make the first move the pool of people available to you is drastically smaller than if you can ask out anyone you want. Bonus: you attract men who are comfortable with confident women.

Set all games aside. No playing hard to get or the three day rule. You can't do one thing and expect to get another.

Be scrupulous about communicating in a way that is clear, honest, direct. This reduces hurt feelings and misunderstandings. Also, the clearer you are about what you want, the easier it is for what you are looking for to find you.

Remember the importance of consent. Don't assume. Ask. If you believe asking takes the fun out of things, ask with imagination. Trust me. Nothing is sexier than consent.

Remember the importance of boundaries. State them clearly. If you are not comfortable or if you are not sure or if something doesn't feel right, the word you are at a loss for is *"no"*.

Don't let online dating mess with your head. It lends a false sense of abundance. Just look at all those people you could be reaching out to. There are many good people out there but it's extremely hard — needle in a haystack hard — to come across someone you truly click with. Invest the time and energy every relationship demands. The sense that *"there are many fish in the sea"* leads to carelessness, regret, and eventually hopelessness and disenchantment.

Most important point for last: safety first. Go on dates in public places. Let someone know where you are and with whom. Don't ever override an inner voice that suggests you are not safe.

How Do You Take Things Slow?

I make time for myself. I want to spend every possible minute with this person, but making time for myself is essential.

It's so easy to get caught up in the dazzle and the chemistry, especially if everything is feeling so thrilling and so good.

As much as it might seem like the other person is setting the pace, a dynamic between two people is a system so it helps to identify how I might be contributing to the speed of the relationship.

I make time for myself to consider the following:

What do I want? Do I know what the other person wants?

When I feel *"things are moving too quickly"* what am I afraid of? Is it commitment? Fear of falling in love? I don't want to misrepresent my intentions, nor push away what I want the most.

Once my insides are clear, I communicate as clearly as I can. Are we in the same reality? Are we perceiving things similarly? Do we want the same things?

I work on expressing, establishing and enforcing my limits. What am I ready to give? Where do I want to say no? (Code red: am I saying yes to keep the other happy?)

If we are on the same page and communicating clearly, we can make some decisions together. We might decide to see each other less often. To make dates shorter. We might pace ourselves on big milestones. We might both focus on now, instead of alluding to the future.

The questions I am most careful with are: does this person feel perfect for me? Like I've found my soulmate? This indicates I need to slow down, take time to get to know him, align fantasy with reality.

The only way to identify the role I play, recognize what I need and articulate it, and set the perfect pace is to step out of the whirlwind and noise of being swept off my feet and listen to myself.

How Do You Know if You Can Trust Someone?

Trust feels like it's in others but it's a feeling so it's really inside of me.

Once I trust myself all I do is notice how others behave and completely trust that they will continue to behave in a way that is consistent to what they have shown me.

Expecting anyone to change or to suddenly behave in the way that I need — rather than in the way they are — hurts me and is therefore not very considerate of me (towards me).

This lack of self-compassion comes from an absence of trust in myself.

In other words, I know that I can really trust someone by trusting me and noticing their behavior, not only towards me but towards everyone.

How Do You Not Let Your Girlfriend's Past Bother You?

Look. My partner's past bothers me.

It bothers me!

It bothers me that he was ever (*augh!*) madly in love with someone else, that he (*my gawd*) had sex with other women, that he (*ooof*) shared really, mega-important, life altering things with people other than me.

Sometimes I feel a flash of jealousy but more than that I think about this (*oh no brain don't do that*) and feel rumpled and disordered and uncomfortable. Ugh.

Just ugh.

But then I sit back and consider the person that he is. He is this wondrous, emotionally intelligent, adroit, gentle, thoughtful, loving human in large part because of the experiences that have shaped him.

In a very real, direct sense it's thanks to other women that he is such an unbelievable catch. And now, yours truly (me) gets to reap the benefits of the extremely wide variety of skills he has picked up along the way.

(Thank you, ladies!)

And that's how I don't let his past bother me.

BEFORE...

BEFORE...

THE WONDER OF RIGHT NOW

LEARNNG TO LOVE

How Do I Make Sure I Never Have Needs?

Every human has needs. For sleep, for water, for food; for love, connection, respect, trust; for relevance, independence, learning, creating.

Needs are normal, essential — not just to stay healthy but to remain alive.

Self-care is the ability to listen, identify and satisfy my own needs. To soothe myself if I am anxious, to keep myself company when I'm alone, to sleep when I'm tired.

If along the way I ever learned that I should not have needs, that other people's needs were more important than mine, I will always associate needing with a sense of discomfort, with shame. How self-absorbed of me to need anything. How selfish.

How painful, to want to get rid of something you can't not have.

What if the secret to happiness, to peace, was to accept? To accept that I, like everyone else, have needs? What if I learned to stop judging them, if I stopped judging myself for having them?

What if I recognized that anyone who declares I need too much wants me to ignore my needs and meet theirs, at the expense of my own?

We can (and should) take responsibility to meet many of our needs. For others we are interdependent, social beings who learn to communicate, and create relationships.

Needs make us human. Their existence impels us to relate, to ideate, to make, to grow. If we denied them, if we managed to obliterate them, we would not survive.

How To Fight Better

I keep an eye on my ego. She wants to be right, wants to win, wants to be responsible for nothing. I recognize relationships are a system and everyone plays a role in how things unfold. Instead of spelling out how I was wronged I look for the role I played in anything that didn't go right.

I recognize the existence of more than one perspective, and more than one preference. We can be different, do things differently and like different things and both be right.

I stay away from any behavior that could be punishing: yelling, insults, the silent treatment, keeping score, taking revenge, tit for tat, freezing someone out. Instead, I stay present and work at making sure we both feel safe.

I remain aware of expectations and assumptions (they are so sneaky!). These exist only in my head, which means I am operating from a place the other can neither know nor see. This usually looks like us believing that we are talking about one thing when really we are talking about another; or like one of us being disappointed at something we never knew we were supposed to do.

Boundaries, boundaries, boundaries. Being aware of my limits and expressing them is a constant practice. Having limits is not selfish. Having limits is human.

Acknowledge everyone comes with a past. If their reaction (or my reaction) to something is completely out of proportion to what is taking place, it's likely something in the present has activated something from the past. Understanding, tolerance and compassion help navigate unexpected storms.

It's so powerful to take a break. *Can we go on a walk and talk more later? Can we sleep on this? Can we hit the pause button on this specific thing and talk about something else?* I try to avoid talking when I know I can't think.

And perhaps most importantly: nothing good comes out of being critical, nitpicking, nagging, noticing the worst or wondering how I can "catch" someone doing something wrong. If I am in a relationship with someone it means I believe in them. I exercise assuming the best and noticing all the things they do well — their thoughtfulness and generosity and talent and big heart. Thank you. Thank you so much for loving me.

How Can I Forgive Without Resentment?

When someone hurts me, my mind — my thoughts — does one of two things.

The first is, my thoughts can rile me up. They can dwell on the issue and make it bigger. *He did this, he knew it was going to hurt me, he did it anyway, he tried to hide it, how could he. How could he?*

Or, my thoughts can calm me down. I can dwell on the issue and sow understanding into my own thought patterns. *Maybe this was just an error in judgment and he didn't think it through. He wanted to be honest but decided not to, to avoid a fight, which is a very human thing to do.* Many mistakes are not done on purpose, not done with an intent to hurt.

We are all doing the best we can.

When my thoughts go to making the issue bigger I turn them towards making the issue smaller.

I remind myself that forgiving is a strength. It makes my relationships more resilient, and makes me more resilient too.

Forgiveness takes time. It takes practice. Ultimately it is about making the future better, lighter, free of the burden of anger or bitterness. It's really a gift to myself.

FORGIVENESS TAKES PRACTICE.

THIS or this

Quid Pro Quo

I don't like the feeling that my relationships are a quid pro quo. This to me is cramped, monitored, rigid, strained, scarce, controlled. From this place I don't know how to get somewhere that's healthy and loose and light and unconcerned.

Instead, I think about a long, broad swath of time. I think about a wide territory of changing circumstances, like a mountain range. If I am with a friend I consider important and I am in a position to give, I do. I lean on the knowledge that if the roles were reversed, she'd do the same for me.

Trust Issues

If I have trust issues, I assume the worst, am hyper-vigilant, default to suspicion and catastrophic thinking and conclude people are sooner or later going to hurt me.

This means I protect myself from others, constantly look for evidence of what I already believe to be true, and am extremely reactive. Things that are easily dismissed by someone who trusts can become big arguments for someone who can't.

Most humans will at some point have trust issues. This is because trust issues are what happens to people who have been hurt, betrayed or abandoned — not just by a significant other but by parents, family, friends.

We have all been hurt.

Trust issues can be fleeting rather than permanent, and can be overcome. We can learn how to better process what has happened to us, to accept every relationship implies a risk worth taking, and can join forces with the people who love us to heal from what we have been through.

I have never — not ever — met an individual completely free of red flags. Relationships are fraught. Love makes us vulnerable. Opening our heart and exposing ourselves can be scary as shit.

The fact that we are out there at all fills me with wonder. I am in endless awe of our spirit and our resilience.

Balancing Act

Life is a balancing act.

It's normal for me to have habits, hobbies, interests, goals, for my days to have a rhythm, and for it all to become disrupted as I make room for a relationship. Relationships are incredibly important, the fabric of life, and they take up a lot of time, energy and attention.

As weeks go by, I witness just how much I've pushed aside, consider and recalibrate.

Some things get lost or stored in the back of the closet — this is natural. In exchange for this I gain so much. Love and companionship and the new world that is another person. The chance to explore things I never knew or thought to consider interesting.

I take a good, broad view of my inner landscape, because this is where the real answers are. How do I feel? Am I being compassionate towards myself? Am I receptive to this new relationship, giving it an open heart? Am I feeling expansive, or am I feeling resentful? Is my lifeview widening or narrowing?

Am I taking care of myself, or neglecting myself? Am I being too rigid and unreceptive to the beautiful things I have been given? Am I gaining a new perspective, or am I losing an important part of who I am? Am I spending time with the people who are important to me?

And to me, the question that allows for all the other questions to be answered: am I making sure I have time to myself?

I regularly check-in, with receptivity, with compassion. I recalibrate accordingly.

IT'S A BALANCE

Should I Put Myself First and Live My Best Life?

This question glorifies the process, making it sound instant — like releasing my wrists from heavy iron shackles — and magical, like running with translucent, white wide-legged pants towards a pink orange sunset.

There is nothing inherently wrong with this visual (or the outfit). It's just that my experience is that the process can be painful and difficult and if I don't know that going in, I feel discouraged, disheartened or like I'm not doing it right.

It's hard to stick with something that makes me feel this way if I am not prepared for it.

Deciding to put myself first is massively uncomfortable and slow and takes real commitment. It means continuously setting boundaries and often completely recalibrating relationships with people I once wanted more than anything to keep close to me.

It means doing things I don't really want to do, like choosing healthier things to eat and going out less and getting up early and exercising discipline.

It means realizing that there is no way out from taking full responsibility.

It means being willing to always carry a little bit of guilt and a sense that I have failed others.

It means practicing needing less approval and more asking myself what it is that I really want to do.

It's extremely hard to break the habits of attempting to be liked or thought highly of.

These things take a lifetime of messing up and being willing to start over.

To answer the question, what happens is that I no longer feel lost, listless or resentful. The people I want to be with want to be with me. And I am in full possession of the only life I'll ever have.

The Work You and Your Significant Other Do Together

Chapter 5

Dating

What's Your Perfect First Date?

My perfect first date would be with someone I already like, rather than someone I don't know.

Maybe with someone I've talked to a lot but never met in person. Someone I've already established a connection with — but, what would it be like, to actually be in your presence? Would hanging out confirm or completely change what I suspect?

He'd be standing there early one morning holding my coffee. Before walking up to him my brain would roar the verdict in my ears: *Confirm.*

We'd walk and talk with both ease and nervous energy. We'd sit on the grass in the park. He would be interesting to talk to, and a good listener. It's hard to find both in the same person, I think.

We'd get hungry (wait — is it lunchtime already?) and scavenge for a place to eat. We'd buy a chicken sandwich and sit on a sidewalk bench. That sandwich would be unwrapped slowly and would have to aggressively arrest his attention.

Good food demands you stop everything and do nothing but savor it and a perfect first date would have to have that kind of food.

We'd lose track of time or feel like it went by too fast. We'd move things around to make room, just so we can "finish" talking.

A perfect first date eats up the day like a non-native plant that takes over everything.

In the late afternoon we'd return to the coffee shop where the date first started and shuffle our feet. *It was so great to finally meet you*, we would mumble. What a great day.

I'd walk back to my place with a storm inside my chest. *What was that? And, what do I do with it? I don't know. I don't know.*

Many perfect dates would follow that first one. We will kiss someday. We will have dinner outside. We will set aside and fill entire days with nothing. We will meet each other's people.

We will someday find a finer balance where it no longer feels like this vine is wrapping itself around everything.

But that first date is just this. Wonder. A tension. Total internal disarray. And the perfect chicken sandwich.

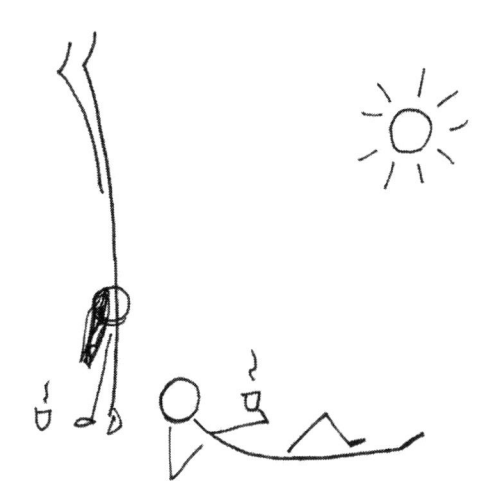

I Have a Crush on a Girl I See on the Bus. What Do I Do?

"Hello.

"You and I get on the same bus, and I would love to get to know you better.

"Here is a list of places along our bus route that might be fun to explore." (Hand her a piece of paper.)

"Would you like to pick one so that on an appointed day we can get off the bus together, sip something and get a chance to talk?"

(Drawing by Dan Roam, which maybe someday you can show her.)

Is Love a Social Construct?

Marriage is a social construct. So is playing hard to get, monogamy, and the sense that a person can belong to you.

Religion is a social construct, and tradition, and family, and prayer — much of what we believe in, how we behave and the norms we follow.

Money is a social construct, and currency and the letter of the law.

Mondays are a social construct, as is noon and the fact it's past my bedtime.

Things we build are social constructs, like architecture and language, and things we create, like art, music, literature, entertainment.

Whatever we decide to wear as a singular form of self-expression is a social construct and so is every bit of the culture we evolve in, unfold in, establish ourselves in, give ourselves over to in an attempt to belong.

Much of who we think others are and even who we think we are is a social construct, and everything I do to get you to like who you think I am.

This is not to say these things do not really exist or are not important or valuable, but rather that they are all true because we as a society have decided they are.

I think it's quite possible there is only one thing that's objectively real, and that is love.

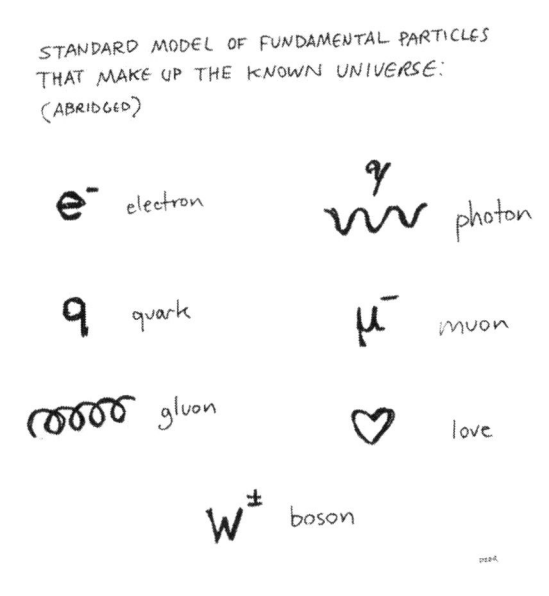

STANDARD MODEL OF FUNDAMENTAL PARTICLES
THAT MAKE UP THE KNOWN UNIVERSE:
(ABRIDGED)

e^- electron

γ photon

q quark

μ^- muon

gluon

♡ love

$W^{\pm}$ boson

What Is Often Falsely Portrayed in Pop Culture?

Relationships. It perpetuates all the things we do in relationships that hurt and confuse us.

Love is not a fairy tale. There is no savior, no soulmate, no perfect member of a royal family. Successful relationships recognize that we are flawed and messy and that we have to learn how to communicate. Expecting another person to just know how I feel is the kind of expectation that crushes a relationship.

We are not a scrap of a person looking to complete itself. We are fully responsible for ourselves and the management of our emotions. No one else can "make us happy"; no one else can assume responsibility for our jealousy or our apathy or our tendency to procrastinate.

If anyone thinks this is simply not romantic, consider the stunning beauty in the fact that we are not lost, broken fragments of anything. I am whole, and so are you.

If anyone thinks it's selfish to be completely responsible for ourselves and the management of our emotions, consider how selfish it really is to expect someone else to do for me what I need to do for myself. Why should any part of me — in particular the most crucial parts like my joy and sense of direction — be someone else's job?

The best, most solid relationships are built in increments, step by step, with what we do day in, day out, rather than in one grand gesture. Grand gestures lend the relationship a wide swinging pendulum feeling that anything can happen, instead of a sense that I am safe, self-possessed, with you.

Relationship Myths

I can't help who I'm attracted to.

Soulmates are something you find.

If you are not certain, this person is not The One.

Emotional unavailability just means I have work to do — I can make someone love me.

I should play hard to get because men are hunters.

If things are not perfect, you just haven't met The One.

The One is responsible for making you happy.

Everything suddenly falls into place.

It's supposed to feel like in the movies.

Happily ever after is a given.

If it's not easy, it's not meant to be.

Never go to bed angry.

Jealousy means love.

Possessiveness means love.

You should do everything together.

True love means no boundaries.

True love is unconditional.

True love means grand gestures.

True love means you never fight.

If you love someone, you can change who you are.

True love means you shouldn't need therapy.

Misunderstandings mean this person is not The One.

You should just know what I want.

If it feels like a roller coaster, that's because it's passion.

What makes relationships work is compatibility.

All you need is love.

Love conquers all.

Is Being Opinionated Unattractive on a First Date?

What is or is not attractive is subjective. Different people are attracted to different things.

Dating is the process by which I determine if I like who I meet, just the way they are, and if they like me.

If I am opinionated, what I need to do on a first date is be opinionated. That way, the people who remain interested like me for who I am (rather than for who I am not).

If they don't like that I am opinionated, they are not for me, and the earlier I determine this, the better.

No person is right for everyone, and that is a wonderful, liberating thing.

The Opposite of "Emotionally Unavailable"

Clarity: I know what I want, and what I want is you.

A lack of interest in drama, inconsistency, and unpredictability.

The ability to set boundaries.

Alignment between what I say and what I do.

Clear communication.

Being a good listener.

Trust. No one is doubted, questioned, required to prove anything.

The sense that I am safe.

An understanding that relationships are not perfect.

An ability to disagree.

Commitment: this is rough and we will work it out.

You are not required to read someone's mind.

Connection everywhere, not just during sex.

A hunger to work on ourselves.

A steady sense that I am worth loving and deserve a relationship that is respectful, peaceful, and happy.

Do You Forget How To Kiss After a Dry Spell?

The human brain has very sticky memory storage areas. This is where it stashes things it interprets as necessary for survival: ice skating, riding a bicycle, snowshoeing, thwacking a ball with a bat.

It also has non-sticky memory storage areas where it "keeps" things it doesn't feel it needs. If you learn a language and don't use it it will become rusty quite quickly. I guess our brains figure that if we are not speaking in French every day, we probably won't.

We never forget kissing. We can kiss a lot, then not kiss for a decade or more. One day there she is, curls splayed against the beige floor cushion, expecting you to kiss her.

Your kiss unfurls before you like it was always there, like it never left you, like we knew all along we'd need this again some day and kept it in a special place, safe and warm and carefully wrapped in rainbow tissue paper that could be torn open one sunny Saturday morning seventeen years from now.

Our brain knows we need to kiss to survive.

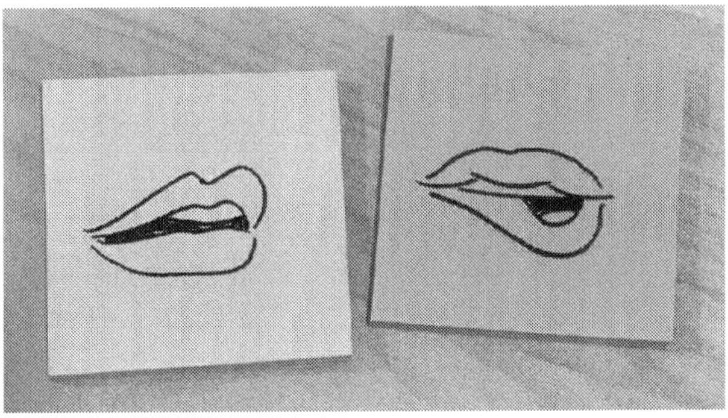

Is Feeling Attracted to More Than One Person Akin to Polyamory?

Monogamy means I am in a romantic relationship with one person at a time. It does not mean I have somehow become unable to see the bounty, the abundance, and the undeniable, varied beauty of others.

Of course I am attracted to more than one person. Being attracted to another man — or another woman, for that matter — does not make me polyamorous. What it makes me is human.

What Is "Negging"?

"Negging" is a pick-up technique. Here is how it works:

Someone makes a backhanded compliment with the intent of making the other person feel self-conscious. This shakes their confidence and leaves them feeling intrigued, hungry for attention or approval.

It's extremely not cool to be hurtful, put someone down or make fun of them, for any reason. A person who resorts to this deserves neither your attention nor your curiosity.

Are "Situationships" Necessarily Toxic/Unwelcome?

"Toxic" refers to something poisonous, harmful, sometimes lethal.

A "situationship" refers to a dynamic between two people that has not been defined.

If you are intertwinkling your life with another but are not calling it anything, have not committed to anything, if you are having sex but it doesn't feel like "friends with benefits", because, I dunno, then you've got yourself a situationship.

How does said situationship make you feel? Do you feel light, like there is no pressure, like leaving things open is cool, like *there is no rush, we can define this later*?

Or do you feel like, *look, I know what I want and it's you*, like *I want more than this*, like *I am feeling anxious and frustrated in this ambiguous hell of my own creation*?

If it makes you feel buoyant, then it's not toxic. If it makes you feel stressed and on edge, then that can't be good for you.

I will add one important thing that you won't really listen to until it's too late but I will attempt to get you to save yourself anyway: just because you're "keeping it cazh" and not calling it anything does not inoculate you from the pain of dissolving it.

How do you "break up" if you were never a thing? It can make "leaving" more — not less — painful because of the lack of delineation.

Tragically, I have never been good at situationships. Ambivalence makes me feel like I'm wasting my time, and I find decisiveness supremely attractive. That said, just because something doesn't work for me doesn't mean it can't be just right for someone else.

What Is a Fling?

A fling is a "relationship" — a dynamic? a situationship? — intended to be fun and light and physical and sexual and effervescent and filled with mutual attraction and the opposite of commitment.

A fling lacks anything that smacks of a future. You don't build. You don't create. You don't bring your friends and families together. You don't make long term plans. You don't have deep conversations. Things tend to be spontaneous, and not particularly thoughtful.

You see each other, sometimes frequently, but your lives do not mix.

Flings are really fun if participants are clear about the fact that what they are involved in is just for now.

The problem is that hand in hand with a fling is often a lack of clarity, a sense that since this is just a fling you don't really need to bother with communication, that you can "play it loose" and "just go with the flow" — which typically results in someone getting hurt.

What do I want? Am I being clear about it, or am I pretending I want something "light" hoping it becomes something serious? Is what I want in line with what the other person wants?

If we want the same thing, a fling can be flung.

Final warning: *"we will not get emotionally involved"*, *"let's agree we won't fall in love"* and *"we are strong and independent and can do whatever we decide"* is all well and good.

Just remember our hearts are not governed by the decisions our brains make, or by the pacts we make with others. We can make a deal to not get emotionally involved and immediately proceed to getting emotionally involved (oh, heart).

Is this hurting me? Am I hurting someone? If so, this is not a fling. This is an impending disaster, and it's time to walk away.

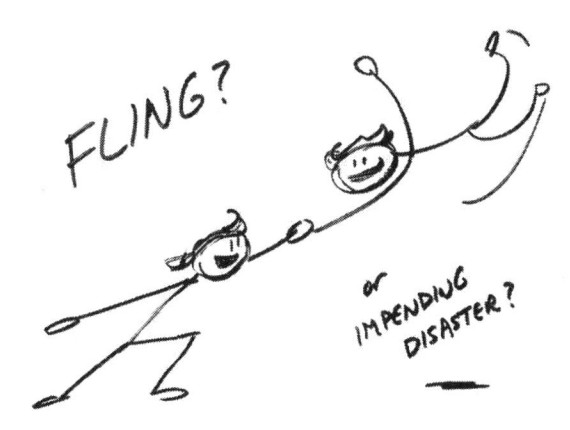

Should I Give Up on Relationships and Just Have Sex?

I have an unfortunate condition there is no known cure for. It's called (ugh) being human.

The inevitable, inexorable, unavoidable symptoms include making mistakes and not learning from them, and feeling like I can't get anything right.

Also, messing up relationships and feeling convinced I will never figure out another person (or myself).

Also, I will experience loneliness, self-doubt, pain and a sense I am not enough and can never do enough.

Also, I will frequently fail, feel like I have no purpose and wonder who I am, what I want and what the heck I am doing.

But, there is a twist. If I feel all these things — exasperation, inadequacy, isolation, and an impending sense that I just want to give up — it means I am doing it right.

If you want to throw in the towel, I don't blame you at all, but know this: If you want to throw in the towel you are doing something right.

Do Most Men Have Commitment Issues?

Commitment can be terrifying.

It's the place where I can get tied down, feel suffocated, trapped, lose my independence, lose myself.

It's where I can get hurt, where I am at my most vulnerable.

It's where I can get abandoned.

It's where I can fail.

It's where I can feel at my most inadequate, my most powerless.

It's where I worry that maybe there is something else out there I'm missing out on, where I consider that maybe I am choosing the wrong thing to commit to.

Most humans have been hurt in previous relationships and/or have never witnessed a healthy, happy relationship. As such, "commitment issues" are incredibly common, and unrelated to gender.

If a Woman Never Compliments Me, Is She Not Interested?

Humans are really weird. We spend so much time and so much energy and so many thought cycles holding back.

What if the other person thinks I am too interested? What if the other person thinks I am too eager? What if the other person thinks I am desperate?

I have so many emotions. So much attraction! So much enthusiasm! I feel thrilled! What should I do? Where do I put all this? How do I hide something this unwieldy?

We take whatever we are feeling and we cloak it. We disguise it. We conceal it. We use camouflage and dissimulation and attempt to act nonchalant.

Incredibly, we aim for the most awful thing: an absence of emotion.

We strive to appear indifferent.

Imagine, being given the gift of color and doing everything possible to seem gray. Aloof, when what I really feel is electric.

So, I don't know. If you are dating someone and they are not complimenting you, sure. It could be that they are not into you. It could be that they are not in the habit of giving compliments. Or, it could mean she is trying to play it safe.

There is one way to know for sure and that is to ask. *"I really like you. Do you like me too?"* Best of all, asking requires exposing how you feel. Because, who wants to live under all this pretending?

Nervous To Kiss You

Imagine that I have experience riding a bike.

One day, I find myself on a new road. I approach the first hill.

There we are, my bike and I, perched on the very top, ready to dash all the way down.

I'm nervous. I've never been here before. I expect it to be marvelous, but there is always an element of unpredictability (which adds to its splendor).

A lot of what I am identifying as nerves is actually nervous anticipation. The thrill. The wind in my hair. The whoosh in my ears. The grip. The hurtle and dive.

It's not the bike. It's the hill.

What Is the Difference Between "Red Flags" and "Flaws"?

A red flag in a relationship is behavior that indicates the presence of a problem that might be too big to deal with; something seemingly small that is actually of greater significance.

Does the guy you have just begun dating blame everyone else for everything that has gone wrong in his life? This is a red flag for someone who is not accountable for his actions.

A flaw in a relationship is an indication that the relationship is not perfect.

If at any point anyone believed or expected that it would be, that's a red flag.

Eggplant

I liked him so much. I liked everything about him, except he liked eggplant, and I did not.

When we went to restaurants we'd order a couple of dishes and split them. He'd gravitate towards the dish with the eggplant and I'd say nothing.

I'd say nothing, again and again.

Saying nothing was a lot more subtle than wanting to please him: I think I just wanted everything to be easy, and in doing so neglected myself.

I got so tired of always getting the eggplant.

This is how he pushed and crossed my limits every time we ordered food: not knowing he was doing so. This is how I eventually got resentful of always ordering what he wanted, and never a meal I could enjoy.

When I don't clearly state what I want I not only leave it unsaid. I encourage the other person to be unable to deliver.

After a First Date, What Makes You Want a Second?

I pay close attention to how I feel after the date.

Am I second guessing myself? Do I feel anxious? Do I feel drained? Am I relieved it's over? Do I feel like I just checked off a chore?

Was everything really fun, but somehow I feel empty?

Or do I feel light, relaxed, excited, curious?

Maybe the date wasn't "perfect". But, when I think about next weekend or the weekend after that, is he in it?

When I feel interested in going out with someone again, it's less about the other person, and more how the other person made me feel.

Many things about the date can delude me into believing it went well but there is something about checking in with my own state of mind that does not mislead me.

What Does Holding Hands Feel Like?

I know there's a buffet with many delicious things available to me — and I love them all — but gawd I love holding hands.

I love the gentle, tight clasp, the warmth, the rhythm, the cadence loop.

The fit. My god — the fit.

The skin. Warm and soft and rough and alive.

We are alive.

Look at us, walking in the sun.

I love the sway, the sweep, the give, the lock, the firm, transient possession, the belonging.

I love the touch.

I love that I fidget and you subtly tighten the grip like an unspoken *no Dushka where do you think you're going.*

I love that I'm talking but half-paying attention to what I'm saying. Because really all I want is to feel your fingers threaded into mine, alternated, yours mine yours mine yours.

You and me I think it's you and me. You and me.

I don't know why people stop holding hands. It's like we run out of time to do the very things that never took any time at all.

Does Dating Guys With Relationship Experience Matter?

A person with relationship experience has left behind the illusion of fairy tale love. More *"let's work through what happened"*, less *"if this isn't easy, we're not meant to be".*

They know to ask, rather than make assumptions. More *"what would feeling loved look like to you?"*, less *"nothing I do seems to be enough".*

They know how to communicate. More *"I am feeling hurt and would love to talk when I sort myself out".* Less *"nothing's the matter".*

They spell out their expectations. More *"my birthday's next month. Can I tell you how I want to celebrate?"*, less disappointment.

There is more noticing of the good instead of the bad. More *"I love how focused you are when you work"* less *"you never pay attention to me".*

They know how to set boundaries. More *"when I feel stressed I like to talk through things but don't want advice. Could you just listen?",* less sighs of exasperation.

They know how to respect boundaries. More *"if you need time alone, just call me later!"* less *"if you need time alone you don't want to be with me".*

They know how to apologize. More *"what I did was not OK and I am so sorry."* Less *"I'm sorry you feel that way".*

They listen and recognize another perspective. Less *"don't be so sensitive"* more *"I can see how that must have felt uncomfortable".*

There is less of a tendency to put themselves at the center of every story. More *"you must be so busy"* and less *"if you didn't reply to my text you've lost interest".*

There is evidence of self-care. More *"I'm going to bed early because I have a big day tomorrow",* less *"poor decisions make good stories".*

There is enthusiastic support for growth and evolution. More *"I want for you what you want for you"* and less *"if you do well I will lose you".*

The Sprout

Love, even big love, is like a seed, a sprout, full of potential, power, life.

If you feed it you get a jungle, rich in its abundance and biodiversity.

You feed it with your attention, with your care, with self-awareness and generosity of spirit. You feed it with small, consistent acts.

If you don't feed it, it will die.

You let it go hungry with an absence of attention, with the small choices you make to turn away when it requires something from you.

Love starves when you take it for granted, which is what we do when we demand it shoulder the burden of all the things life throws at us.

Chapter 6

Commitment and (Maybe) Marriage

Am I in Love?

Ah, yes. Love. What a catastrophic predicament.

Tell me.

Do you wish you could stop time? Do eight hours with him feel like a minute or two?

When you are with him does it feel like just looking at him is a completely satisfactory activity?

Did he somehow gain easy access to an internal landscape you had not considered sharing?

Do you start missing him three or four minutes before he leaves?

When he's gone, does everything remind you of him?

Does everything feel like a sign? (You like pickles!? I like pickles!)

When you look back at the things that had to align so you could meet, is your conclusion that the only viable explanation is divine intervention?

What is happening to your brain and your body chemistry? Does it feel like you are a human pinball machine?

Are you feeling stressed?

How are you sleeping? Are you tossing around? Do you feel jolted, disrupted?

When was the last time you ate?

What does the world look like? Is color brighter, edges sharper? Does the world seem a more hopeful place?

When you are together, do you feel an astonishing sense of — ease?

Do you laugh a lot?

Is your time together fulfilling, even when you are not doing much?

Do you keep a list of a thousand things that would make the perfect gift for him? Another list with all the things you've already done that you want to do again so you can do them with him? Another with things you need to get around to doing together, just as soon as you can get your hands off him? Is his happiness on your list of priorities?

Do you want to know everything, everything about him?

Do you want to introduce him to everyone?

Are you planning? Are you thinking about your future — next week, next month, next year — with him in it?

Do you want to be better at everything?

Are you in total disbelief? Like, how is it that I get to be with him?

I wouldn't dare diagnose an emotion in someone else, but I can tell you that when I suspect I might possibly be in love, this is what it feels like.

What Does It Mean To Grow in a Relationship?

There are two kinds of relationships.

In one, everyone else's needs come before my own. I need and want things I never express because I am afraid they will reveal too much about me or classify me as a burden.

This means connection is scarce, I feel unseen, and am full of resentment and anger. I feel exhausted and misunderstood. My underlying belief is that to love well I have to sacrifice myself.

This environment is akin to placing myself in survival mode and does not allow for growth.

In the second kind of relationship, I work on myself. I learn to express boundaries, which in turn grants me safety and allows me to be more open. This openness is how I can be seen and heard and in turn can hear and see another.

I can have difficult conversations and make room for my own wants as this is how I give the best of me to others.

As we each work on ourselves we have the space to be honest, to be vulnerable, to explore what we want.

We become better, not just for each other, but better people — better at communicating, at listening, at taking responsibility.

Love is not sacrifice. It's not something to endure. It does not come at the cost of my peace of mind. Love is self-awareness and wonder. This is what it means to grow in a relationship.

When Is the Right Time To Say I Love You?

I have bad news and I have good news.

The bad news is there is no right time to say I love you in a romantic way. *"I love you"* is a leap, a risk, an act of faith, and what if I ruin everything with this coil of words I have pushing their way out of my chest? What if you think it's too soon?

Now, the good news.

There is no bad time to say I love you in a romantic way. Saying it to me feels like a relief, like I should not be concealing this, this is something you've got to see. Because otherwise I have this enormous thing right here sitting between us, this beautiful beast that affects everything, that changes everything, and neglecting to talk about it seems to me to be a huge disservice to all three of us.

How Do I Ask "Where Is This Going" Without Blowing It?

It takes two to determine the trajectory of a relationship — no one person can hold the answer — and I am half of that equation.

To have this conversation, I make sure we are both in a peaceful place. I find a moment that's clean and bright, when we are not fighting, not resentful, not angry, not upset, not lashing out.

I make sure that what I say next does not sound like a complaint or a demand, or like what I want is something he owes me or better give me. I want to speak from the best lit place inside my heart.

Then I say something like *"I really like my life with you in it. When I imagine my future, you are there. I want to know if you feel the same way."*

Of course this is frightening. But it scares me more to live in the shadows of what I wish for myself, in a world where I'm hopeful, but always waiting, in a dank place where others hold all the answers to what my only life will look like.

Expressing my needs without equivocation or drama either delivers what I want or clears my path towards the exit — so I can make a clean getaway from any place that holds nothing for me.

Do Friends Who Become Lovers Ever Last?

Sex. It's so distracting.

I meet someone and feel a rush of chemistry and my body feels effervescent and my brain spins out fantasies.

This feels delicious. Clearly this indicates this man is the one, a knight on a white horse. He will protect me. He will save me. I mean, look at him. He's so dashing.

When the dust settles and I shake myself out I take a good look at him and realize the person I fell for was the man I created, rather than the person he is.

Who he is is not necessarily bad. Just no match to my expectations.

No one is.

A friend is different. I take the time to get to know him. He gets to know me. We see each other's highs and lows and when our friendship begins to evolve and becomes something more, the person I'm falling for actually exists outside of my imagination.

Friends who become lovers are often on more solid ground.

DEAR

How Does One Resolve Being in Love With Two People?

My heart has a very specific, vertical architecture: I cannot be in love with more than one person at a time.

But, it would be egocentric for me to assume that my experience has to be everyone's experience, that what is true for me must be true for everyone.

Many, many people can and do fall in love with more than one person, at which point they have the following options:

To resolve they should be with one of them, and carry the love for the other around without doing anything about it. Just because you love does not mean you have to act on it.

To resolve to be with both of them. To talk to them both and have a relationship with both of them if everyone is comfortable with this arrangement.

To lie to one or both of them, and have both a relationship and a lover.

To decide to be with neither of them (which is frequently the outcome of option number three).

What Does Having the Same Values Mean?

Values are what matter to me the most: they define how I want to live my life. Having the same values as my partner means we see life unfolding in ways that can coexist in harmony.

If one of you feels religion should be at the center of it all, if one of you longs for a life of devotion and the other is largely agnostic (or an atheist), your values are different.

If one of you wants a family and dreams of owning a car big enough for five and the other does not want children, your values are different.

If one of you wants multiple meaningful relationships and the other wants you both to have only one, your values are different.

Values — a common vision for what you are building — help relationships withstand hard times. What they imply is that you are creating something beyond the two of you, something bigger that can hold you together when life gets hard. Life always gets hard.

I Love You Too

When someone says *"I love you"*, I typically respond with *"I love you"*.

I've always found *"I love you too"* or *"I love you back"* to be derivative.

It feels less strong to me, second hand, a by-product, the tentative result of a firm, meaningful, original declaration.

Every *"I love you"* deserves a crisp, fresh start.

What Should I Know Before Getting Married?

You will never "get it right". Not ever. Who do you want to find yourself with when you wake up feeling like you broke something?

Feelings are fleeting. They are more like tumbleweed than like roots. As they come and go, find something more solid to anchor onto.

You don't ever understand yourself. You don't ever understand another. This is where the discovery is, the mystery and the awe.

You don't ever really know what you want. This makes life a winding, possibly pointless adventure. Who do you want to wander aimlessly around with?

You are carrying truckloads of baggage. You can't ever see things as they are. If you have to walk across a field of broken glass while blindfolded, whose arm do you want to be holding onto?

No one is responsible for any of your emotions. You can't expect another to make you happy. You cannot demand that anyone accommodate you feeling jealous or stranded. It also means that for the most part, you do things to yourself.

Loneliness is not the absence of other people. The absence of others is an outside condition. Loneliness is inside. It never works, to repair an inside thing with an outside fix.

No one else can save you from yourself and you cannot help or fix another. If you are expecting marriage to be the answer — well. Every morning you will wake up to find you still have to contend with you.

Marriage is not inoculation against heartbreak.

Marriage is not a guarantee.

In Relationships, How Do We Know Which Risks Are Healthy?

Risk-taking has to do with exposure, with taking a chance.

To identify a healthy risk, I ask myself: Does this risk teach me? Does it test me? Does it push my limits? Does it make me think? Does it widen my perspective? Is it related to my own vulnerability? Does it build my confidence? Will it make my life richer?

Healthy risks in relationships (including my relationship with myself) might look like this:

Tell the truth. Tell yourself the truth. Say yes a lot. Say no like you mean it. Travel. Travel alone. Forgive. Forgive yourself. Defy. Defy fear. Question. Question yourself. Try new things. Try public speaking. Try new food. Set goals — maybe some that seem far-fetched. Fall in love. Quit. Move. Start over. Reconnect with a lost friend. Spend time alone. Do more. Do less. Do what scares you.

To identify an unhealthy risk, I ask myself: Why am I considering this? Am I thinking this through? What could go really wrong? Could this risk provoke violence or cause injury? Could this risk make me sick or cause me to get hurt? Does this risk impair my ability to make the right decision? Does this take me to a place I might not come back from?

Do People Get Hurt in a Healthy Relationship?

Absolutely.

Nobody is perfect. We are human and as such we can be grumpy, clumsy, rude, tactless, ignorant, jump to the wrong conclusions, blame, be critical, get defensive, shut down.

Our behavior hurts the people that we love.

Hurting those we love creates conflict.

Here is the trick, the beautiful trick: what defines a relationship as healthy is not the absence of conflict, but conflict handled well.

Conflict handled well creates opportunities to lovingly navigate that conflict. How we manage conflict is how we make our relationships resilient.

We learn to pause. To become more receptive instead of defensive, more respectful instead of careless, to make room for another person's feelings instead of focusing on our own.

We learn that there are other perspectives, vantage points and ideas beyond ours — that seeing things differently is not an act of aggression or even defiance. This is not war — I just take up room.

We assume responsibility, learn to say we are sorry.

We become more self-aware, learn to set ourselves aside so we can listen. We become better people.

We never stop hurting those we love, or feeling hurt, because we never stop being human.

I Get Attached Too Easily. What Can I Do?

I want to love fearlessly and wholeheartedly while taking care of myself and my relationship.

Here are the questions I ask myself in an effort to stay on the right track:

Am I neglecting myself to get this person to love me or think highly of me? Am I misrepresenting who I am or what I like, being unclear about how I feel, neglecting things that are important to me, and being irresponsible? Am I failing to deliver on any promise I made to myself?

Am I at any point believing another person is in possession of something I cannot live without?

Am I in any way measuring my own worth in relation to what this person thinks of me?

Am I expecting this person to be the answer to everything I need?

Do I see that the other person is flawed?

Do we support and encourage each other?

Is either one of us attempting to control the other?

Are we able to have difficult conversations? Do we feel safe when we disagree? Do we listen to each other? Do we communicate clearly?

Does either one of us feel something is off if the level of drama is not at a high?

Do we feel responsible for each other's emotions?

Are we trying to fix or save the other?

Am I spending time alone? Am I doing things just for me? Am I in touch with my own needs?

When I say goodbye do I feel separation anxiety even if I know I will see him in a day or two?

Are we setting boundaries? (If I summarized this whole answer into a single point this would be it. Boundaries are the antidote, which is why I talk about them so much.) When we do, do I feel afraid or guilty?

Am I being hypervigilant, coming at this relationship from a place of fear? Can I remain elastic, trust myself, take a break from all this self-awareness and snuggle and bask in his delicious smell and my tremendous good fortune?

If I don't like my answer to any of these questions, I keep an eye on it. I try not to live in a state of alarm. I don't jump off the deep end with a thermonuclear response.

I just course-correct. I communicate.

"I get overly attached. I have a history of codependency. I really like you, and I don't want to mess this up. Let's work together to create a healthy relationship."

If you are terrified you will mess it up, let me assure you, you will. This is because we are human, and we can't ever "get everything right."

Instead, make the most beautiful, reassuring deal in the world: we will in fact mess this up. When we do, let's keep coming back.

Does "A Movie" Mean He Wants Me to Sleep Over?

Whenever I fret about what someone wants I pause from the wondering and speculating and doubting and thinking and take a step back.

Wait a minute. I've been so busy trying to decode what he wants that I have neglected an important thing.

What do I want?

Do I want to stay the night? How do I feel about this?

Once I have clarity around what I want — or once I've established I'm not yet ready to know what I want — I call him.

"Hi. You invited me over to watch a movie and I'm wondering if you are thinking this means we are going to have sex. Or, if this means I'm going to stay the night. Where are you at?"

To this I might add *"honestly, spending the night at your place sounds wonderful."*

Or, *"the possibility that you might be thinking I'm going to stay over is causing me a bit of stress. I really like you, but I don't think I'm ready. I want to make sure we're on the same page to avoid confusion or disappointment. Are you ok with me coming over to watch a movie, but not having sex?"*

Is "I Would Marry You on One Condition" a Red Flag?

If this condition to marry me is something like *"that you never see your loved ones again"*, *"that from now on you cannot do anything without my express permission"*, *"that from this day forward you have to meet every one of my needs"*, yeah, that would be, beyond a red flag, something to run from.

If the condition instead is *"that we always treat each other with respect"*, *"that we talk regularly about the life we want"*, *"that we recognize each other as flawed"*, *"that we, despite misunderstandings, always keep coming back"*, *"that we believe in each other"*, or *"that we always want what is best for each other"*, then I'd consider his condition quite reasonable.

Fights Are Not Loss

A new relationship is a shimmering thing. The world feels like it just rained and everything is clean.

And one day you fight.

To me, that first fight feels like something broke that I cannot put back together, not even with the assistance of all the king's horses and all the king's men.

What I feel after a first fight, beyond anger or frustration or even fear, is grief. I think I grieve the end of that original, pristine honeymoon phase.

That's how it feels.

Feelings are not facts.

The truth is, beyond being normal, fighting is necessary. It's how I get to build the foundation of this nascent relationship. It's how I decide to commit to us, to this, to being honest, to being afraid, to learning how to be better, to grow.

The fight might feel gigantic but the truth is it doesn't matter. What matters is our willingness to work together despite feeling disappointed, scared or exposed.

Handled well, fights make relationships, and that's the thing to focus on.

What's a Lesson You've Learned From a Past Relationship?

Relationships have always been extremely important to me. This was the sentiment behind me resolving that I would make zero mistakes.

The desperate attempt to get everything perfect resulted in me being both critical and defensive. *No! This was not my fault, see? It was yours!* Otherwise there would be a blemish on my impeccable record, and you would conclude you were better off not loving me.

As it turns out, all relationships, even the best ones, have issues, and conflict. It's not about scrubbing things so they at least appear to be pristine. It's about learning to manage the mess — the natural, inevitable, human mess — with grace and generosity.

Taking responsibility, instead of blaming, means accepting more than one perspective. It means saying I am sorry.

I am certain that there are many mistakes I make that I will make again. But I am getting better at remaining open to the possibility of listening and saying *"you are right"*. Better at taking in how another person feels and saying *"I am sorry"* even when I feel I too was wronged.

This is because I have learned I can say both those things and experience us becoming closer, rather than witnessing the catastrophe I assumed would follow from admitting to my inadequacy.

Your Boyfriend's Relationship With His Kid's Mother

How my boyfriend behaves with his daughter and his daughter's mother shows me clear as day what he's made of. Welcome to a clean line of sight straight into his character.

Watch him closely. Is he emotionally invested? Does he deeply care about how things unfold?

Is he respectful, thoughtful and caring with his family (because that's what they are), even when he sometimes feels trapped, put upon, treated unfairly, used?

Is there an inherent, ever present battle to try to do the right thing, even when the right thing can be hard to define?

How does he meet responsibility? How does he follow through on his commitments? Is he fundamentally a you-can-count-on-me sort of person?

Is he capable of nurturing relationships with people likely to remain in his life forever? Does he cut and run? Does he keep an eye on the long game?

Is he generous? Is he kind? How hard does he try, when things get difficult? How quickly does he get over grudges?

And, the hardest, most telling question. Does his daughter take priority over me?

Look, I want to have my rightful place in his life. And nobody wants complications or drama. It's OK to be upset as you witness his wobbly attempts to navigate things fairly and with grace.

But, look deeper.

It may not seem this way when it feels delicious to be the center of someone's attention, but believe me. If the daughter comes first, if what he's showing me despite the choppiness is a history of being there for the people who matter to him, that's the kind of man I want.

Asking About the Ex

There are two types of questions to ask about someone's ex.

One comes from insecurity, a compulsion to compare, and is unlikely to lead to anything positive. *What did she have that I don't? Did you love her more than you love me?*

The second comes from a place of curiosity. *I want to get to know you better, understand you better, and believe you are what your experiences have made of you. Why did you guys fight? Why did you break up? Do you wish you had done something differently? Are you still friends?*

I listen to the answers carefully. In part because I love good stories, but also I love a person's particular perspective. Is there accountability, responsibility, awareness? What does love teach us?

And, how does what we decide to do for love completely alter the trajectory of our life?

Nothing marks our life as much as love.

I am a fan of asking questions about my partner's past. I think he's a really interesting person, and there is a reason for that: the reason is related to how he's lived his life, the decisions he's made, and the people and places that made him the delightful, thoughtful, caring person he is today.

How To Recover From a Fight

To successfully navigate a storm, the quality of your ship matters. Similarly, the quality of your relationship has a huge impact on your ability to heal after a fight.

Dr. Gottman, a leading relationship scientist, calls this an "emotional bank account."

According to Dr. Gottman, three principles build this emotional bank account:

Getting to know your partner in as much detail as you can. Ask questions, remember the answers, and then ask again, because people evolve and change. Put in other words, be interested in the person that you love.

Visibly notice all the good. Let them know you love them and are proud of them. Thank them often.

Turn towards one another instead of away. Dr. Gottman calls this "bids". Turning towards — asking their opinion, asking questions, collaborating, listening, looking at them — is more important towards building a strong relationship than any grand gesture.

When you fight, repair is any attempt — humor, a joke, a gesture, touch, words — to make things better. Dr. Gottman organizes repair into five categories:

I feel. Examples: *I'm feeling sad. I feel blamed. Please stay in the conversation.*

Sorry. Examples: *Let me try that again. I can see what I did wrong. I really blew it.*

Get to yes. Examples: *I see your point. What worries you? Let's find common ground.*

I need to calm down. Examples: *Can you tell me you love me? Can we take a break? Can we talk about something else for a bit?*

Stop action!: Examples: *Give me a moment. Stop. We are getting off track.*

I appreciate. Examples: *Thank you. I understand. I see what you are saying.*

I find repair incredibly hopeful and radiant. We weigh our relationships down with unreasonable demands we learn from fairy tales and rom-coms. Repair is real. It makes room for the fact that we are human, that we will make mistakes, and that these mistakes, rather than cause irreparable damage, are precisely what we need to make our relationships resilient.

What if Every Relationship Played Out Like a Rom-Com?

If every relationship played out like a rom-com, love would be harmful and women would be colorfully dressed, high-heeled prey.

Men's behavior would be deceitful, threatening and creepy. They would repeatedly ignore our boundaries and force themselves on us.

Men would get arrested for jumping over security lines at airports, for abandoning their cars in the middle of highways, for stalking women and "making them say yes" whenever they said no.

Every wedding would be interrupted, often by the best man.

Women would all be aimless, purposeless, mostly objects waiting around for a man to magically complete us.

If we said *"I don't really want a relationship"* they would conclude we are lying, since rom-coms operate under the assumption that all we want is to be swept off the feet we use to stand on.

Finally, friendship would be a cause for concern. If every relationship played out like a rom-com, chances are pretty good your best friend would tell your wife he's in love with her. The declaration would enchant rather than horrify her.

Is Pestering Similar to Forcing?

Pestering or nagging someone is an attempt to control someone else's behavior.

Attempts to control another do not work. If they ever do, it's for a short time and at a high cost: pestering creates bitterness, anger, resentment, a sense of inadequacy and over time a distancing in my relationship.

Someone full of resentment will retaliate and regain control by — yep — tuning me out, and not doing the thing they are being nagged to do.

Beyond *"please, do not leave your wet towels on the bed"*, I am saying many other things:

I am keeping track of the things you are doing wrong (but not really noticing all the things you do right).

My way is the only way.

My way is better than your way.

There is something wrong with how you do things.

There is something wrong with you.

LIKE THIS, PLEASE.

Why Do We Often Prefer Someone New?

One possible reason is this:

When I like someone I don't know, what I like does not come from who they are (it can't — I've never experienced it) but from inside of me.

The other person becomes a handy mirror for whatever I need to see reflected back at me.

This means that the person I know is real, and the person I don't know is a mirage.

Feeling something for someone I don't know is an optical illusion fueled by my own yearning.

This is why "love" can bloom in an instant, can start fast and furious and certain — *my god, you don't understand, what a connection!* — and as we get to know a person — well. We start liking the person we don't know better.

We are not being fickle. We are believing the fantasy we have weaved for ourselves and then crashing against the reality of them revealing who they actually are.

If I fall in love with a character of my own fabrication, recurring disappointment is something I do to myself.

How Can I Be More Fun?

First. "Fun" is subjective. It means different things for different people. For me, a party or any large, rowdy congregation is not fun.

Fun is a long walk with a bar of salted chocolate. Fun is a cup of tea and a good conversation. Fun is noticing how the flecks in his irises match his yellow sheets.

Second. As implausible as this might sometimes sound, the fact is that any man who is with me chose to be with me. Evidence: he could be with someone else. If he considered someone other than me fun, he wouldn't be here.

Which also means that if I make an effort to be someone other than who I am, I run the risk of becoming more like those other people he found less interesting than me.

Third (and last). More than fun, we all want to feel someone can see us — really see us. So instead of pursuing "fun", I ask questions. I listen. I observe. I challenge myself to see the world through someone else's eyes.

It's the most beautiful part of being in love: the beauty of their polychromatic world, the infinite shades of orange and purple, invisible to me before I met him.

My Boyfriend Stood Me Up.
Do I Get Mad or Say Nothing?

Do you know what I want out of a fight, out of feeling angry or hurt?

I want my relationship to improve.

If my boyfriend stood me up I'd feel disappointed. But if I said anything right away, I might feel an instant of satisfaction at the cost of getting the long term result I want.

So, I'd pause.

I'd begin with reviewing my own actions. What did I do to get here? I rearranged my day to spend time with him. Maybe I should think twice before setting myself aside to see him. You have to make room for a relationship, but, is there something here that needs to be reviewed?

In other words, is some of my anger towards myself?

Next. Sure, I'm hurt. But, beyond that, who is it that I want to be?

It's not OK to stand someone up. But, you know what? I want to be more elastic, to take things in stride, to be better at managing last minute change. I want to learn how to suffer less. What do I need to do to make this kind of infraction matter less?

This is not about giving him a pass or justifying his behavior. This is for me and my own peace of mind. It's for my relationship.

It's an effort to make things lighter in a world that is already difficult and uncertain.

The next day, once I've had a chance to cool off and sort myself out, I talk to him. I don't attack him. Rather, I tell him how I feel. *I feel disappointed when I'm so excited to see you and then don't. It feels like my time doesn't matter.*

I think I also feel scared. Like seeing me has become less important.

I observe his behavior. Does he understand what happened? Does he feel contrite?

Finally, I integrate this incident with the rest of him. Is disrespect and a disregard for my needs a theme? Or is this an isolated event, an anomaly?

If the man before me is committed, steady, loving, thoughtful, solid, that's what matters, and this does not.

Who's Happier: Satisficers or Maximizers?

"Maximizing" and "satisficing" are terms that refer to how people make decisions.

Maximizers look to make the right choices — informed choices that will grant them the maximum possible benefit or utility. They have extremely high standards and tend to take their time making decisions.

Maximizers can be slower, less effective, and suffer under self-imposed pressure to make the best possible decision. They experience more decision remorse, wondering if they made the right call, after deciding.

Satisficers make decisions quickly, and make choices that are "good enough". The term "satisficer" is a combination of the word "satisfying" and "sufficing". They tend to be "satisfied" with what they picked, even if it was not the best possible option.

In a day, we made hundreds of decisions, some small, some large. Maximizing every one of them would leave us incapacitated by our own choices.

Making snap decisions on huge life choices could change the course of our life.

I think people who are happiest are aware of how they make decisions and strive to exist somewhere in the middle — or, are in a relationship where one can balance out the other. You pick the movie. I'll pick the vacation.

What Is the Difference Between Care and Control?

If someone cares about your well-being in a way that is healthy, here is what it looks like:

There is a sense of sovereignty.

You feel free, seen, heard, respected, trusted.

Clear boundaries have been established and observed by both parties. Disagreeing or saying no is not a cause for stress or tension.

Space is both requested and granted without friction, guilt, angst, shame or fear.

We feel responsible for our behavior and do not "own" the behavior of the other.

There is room for each person to have very different opinions and beliefs.

Each person gets to grow and evolve in the way they think is best with the support and company — not the direction — of the other person.

Is Sex Mandatory?

My body is mine. It belongs to me. It belongs to me even if I have a boyfriend. It belongs to me even if I get married.

This is because I am a human, not a possession.

The only person who gets to decide what I do with my body is me.

Sex is not mandatory. It's not something I ever have to do. I can always say no, even if I've said yes in the past.

Sex is fun. It's play. It's joyful. It's something people do to get closer, to feel intimate, to wordlessly communicate. It's something people do because it feels good. Burdening it with a sense that I have to do it weighs down something light and beautiful, crushing it.

It's good to talk about sex at the very beginning of the relationship, and to keep talking about it throughout. Does this feel good? Can I touch you here? I'm curious to try this. I want more sex. I want less sex. What about you? What do you want?

Talking about sex helps keep boundaries clear, in particular because boundaries are capricious and inconstant.

When talking about sex, I can talk about me and my body (that's a boundary) but I cannot make demands on the body of another person (that's control).

I might say *"I love sex. My hope is that it will always be a part of our relationship."*

He might say *"I love sex too! Having sex twice a week feels to me like a reasonable amount of sex. Does this sound reasonable for you too?"*

He can also say *"I don't want sex. I love you very much but do not see sex as a part of our relationship."*

To this, I might say *"I like sex. If you don't ever want to have sex, this to me is a deal-breaker. There is nothing wrong with you. There is nothing wrong with me. We are just not sexually compatible, so we can be friends instead."*

No one can say *"I want sex, so this means you are obligated to give it to me."*

One more thing: sex feels personal, but it's not. If someone does not want to have sex with me, this has nothing to do with me. It does not mean I am unworthy. It does not mean I am not desirable. What it means is the other person does not want to have sex.

To explicitly answer the question: sex is never mandatory.

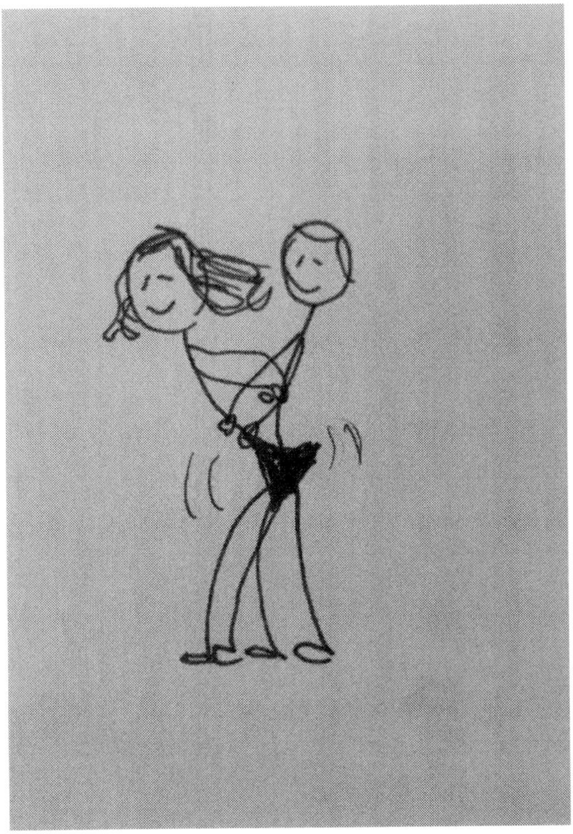

I Feel Butterflies With a Friend but Not My Boyfriend. Why?

When I read your question, the answer springs into my mind instantly. My fingers feel restless and long for a keyboard. Here. Let me just tell you what you are feeling.

But, anything I tell you about your feelings is a projection. I don't know you, so what I tell you is about me, my own feelings, my experience with love and friendship, chemistry and disaster. The fact is I have no authority to dictate to you what you are feeling. It would be presumptuous, and dangerous.

Dangerous because in doing so I would steal your life.

Instead, I encourage you to notice. Notice that you are asking a bunch of strangers to help you identify something only you possess.

Get curious. Abandon judgment. Ask. Why are you doing that? Why are you relinquishing the immense power that you have over your own answers? These questions are incredibly important for you to answer.

Then, notice yourself. What do you feel around your boyfriend and around your friend, within and beyond what you describe in your question?

Spend some time alone and think. Spend some time alone and feel. Spend some time alone and write things down.

The answer — perhaps a glimmering, terrible answer you are afraid to see — is inside you. When you find it, decide what to do about it.

Step into that astonishing power. Step into that terrifying responsibility.

Please don't squander it away. It's the most important thing you will ever have.

THIS YOU'LL NEED TO ~~EXPLORE~~ FOR YOURSELF.
EXPLORE

What Kills Intimacy in a Relationship?

If I expend my energy attempting to control another person — trying to change them, "improve" them, "help" them, "fix" them, "save" them, *"for their own good"* — if I tell them what to do, give them advice, orient them, then all my focus is on *"this is who I want you to be".*

This detracts attention from me seeing who they are, what they need, where they are at, how they are perceiving things, what they are experiencing.

I am in effect creating a wall between me and my ability to see you because I am too busy seeing this other person — who I think you should be.

It's control. Control kills intimacy.

What Should I Do if My Boyfriend Is Keeping Us a Secret?

Whenever I want to make a change in any relationship, I strive for one thing: clarity.

First, I get clear with myself. What do I want? Why is it important? And, what does it look like, exactly?

Then, I get clear with the other person. *"I'd like to meet your friends. It matters to me because I want to feel I am a part of your life. Can we go have dinner with them, maybe this weekend?"*

Of course confrontation can be uncomfortable but stepping outside my comfort zone means feeling uncomfortable and doing it anyway. Otherwise, nothing will ever change.

But mostly, clarity wins.

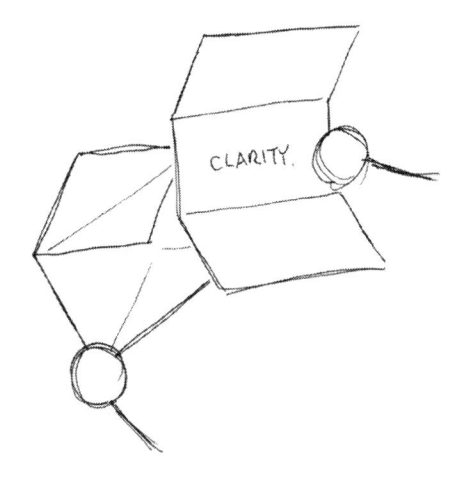

Insecurity

When I was 14-years-old I had a boyfriend who was two years older than me and who I considered an authority on everything. (I mean, he was sixteen.)

One day, shortly after saying he loved me more than anything, he told me he found me overwhelming and that he needed space.

This was like pouring a trickle of poison into a pristine well.

Many of my relationships after that were tangled up in a complicated dance, of me not returning calls or turning down dates, not because I was not interested, not because I was playing games, but because I felt terrified that I would overwhelm the person I was interested in.

I simply did not know how to dispense myself in the right dosage, so the more I cared the more I drew away.

Guys who were interested in me would end up leaving, perplexed, confirming my assumption that what they needed was space.

It wasn't until I decided that I was really rather cool, and that if someone was not interested in me I was interested in me, that I found it in me to stay.

Our perspective is not in how other people see us. It's in how we see ourselves.

Chapter 7

Compatibility

What's the Difference Between Compatibility and Chemistry?

Chemistry is me feeling I am irresistibly drawn to you, that we have some sort of cosmic connection and that I need more of you. It can feel like certainty and is instead mercurial.

Compatibility refers to my ability to coexist with someone free of friction. Incompatibility means living in a constant state of disquiet. Deep incompatibility cannot be overcome and leaves us with the realization that, wow. Love does not conquer all.

Compatible

You want more time with her and she needs space. Who is right?

I can tell you with certainty who is right.

You are right in wanting more time with her. You are not right in thinking she needs too much space.

And, she is right in needing space. She is not right in thinking you are needy.

You each need what you need, and there is nothing wrong with that. What's wrong is assuming the other is wrong, rather than just different from you.

To save you time, you have two choices:

You can accept what the other needs and together work from there.

You can determine you are not compatible, and find someone who needs to give you exactly what you need to receive.

My Boyfriend Called Me Clingy. I Think He's Right. What Can I Do?

I have three things to say.

First, most adjectives are subjective. If I am with a man who craves distance, he might declare me clingy. If I am with one who craves touch and constant contact, he might find I am aloof.

If I defined myself based on how others see me I would always be shape-shifting, and always find me lacking. We assume stillness but the world is a pendulum.

Adjectives — you are fun, boring, clingy, too much — don't speak to our inadequacy. They speak to our compatibility. This is a crucial distinction, because it reminds me there is nothing wrong with who I am.

Second. Do you know what I find fascinating about humans? That we go find people and complain about who they are, when we can instead find the people we claim we want.

If I have a boyfriend and find him clingy, why did I choose him, when the planet offers so many other non-clingy people?

There is a reason I am with this clingy person, which means I am complicit. I am complicit in whatever it is I am complaining about.

So tell me. If you find me clingy and you are with me, what does that say about you?

Third. Self-awareness is an incredibly important part of this equation. So I would ask myself — Is this relationship erasing me? In the company of others, do I neglect myself?

Am I leaving room for me, my identity, my life, my interests, my friends? Am I able to assume full responsibility for me, keeping me company when I am lonely, soothing myself when I am anxious, managing my emotions, making me happy?

If not, this is what I need to work on: loving myself. Caring for myself. Spending time alone. Finding my feet.

This is how I love well, and also how I find who I am. Not in relation to others, but anchored firmly in me.

How Do I Talk My Boyfriend Out of Wanting a Poly Relationship?

The more important something is — the more structural, the more impactful, the harder to reverse — the less room there is for any convincing, persuading, or cajoling.

I can attempt to talk someone into what to order for dinner (and even then they might resent the heck out of me for it) but I cannot and should not talk them into marrying me or having a baby with me.

I cannot talk them in or out of how to architect our relationship.

We have to want similar things.

If I am monogamous and the man I love wants a poly relationship, what I do is hug him, tell him I love him and wish him the best. A man interested in a poly relationship would not be, alas, the man for me.

ALL THE BEST.

Is My Partner the Problem or Is It Me?

Here is how I know if the problem is me:

Am I communicating clearly or do even I have trouble understanding what I want or what I'm saying?

Am I being straightforward, or avoiding conflict?

Am I accountable, or do I blame? Are things always someone else's fault?

Am I expecting him to do something for me I should be doing for myself? (Help me, make me happy, motivate me, solve something for me)

Do I argue over facts or over stories? (*"He didn't reply to my texts"* is a fact. *"I must not be important to him"* is a story.)

Do I frequently complain about "everyone" or "nobody"? (Everyone is driving me crazy today, and nobody understands me.)

Is anything I complain about (such as *"I always feel let down"*) replicating itself across my relationships? If the same problem keeps presenting itself with different people, the problem is me.

Do I make it a point to ask myself *"how did I contribute to this issue?"*

And, when I complain about someone only being concerned about themselves, is what I am saying that they should instead be concerned about me?

How Did Your Relationship Change When You Moved In Together?

Moving in together exposes your true level of compatibility.

When you are dating, visiting, spending a night and then leaving, almost everything is rather sweet. His soft snoring and his penchant for holding you tight. How alert he seems early in the morning.

When you move in together, how I load the dishwasher becomes an item worthy of many conversations. *Wait a minute. Where are all the kitchen towels, Dushka? And, why are the sheets on the bed not tucked in at the bottom? Who can sleep like that?*

Before you know it, little things that you had not noticed — or little things that once brought you comfort, even pleasure — are suddenly a source of irritation.

It's like fluffy, soft things suddenly sprout sharp edges.

For many couples, these points of irritation are difficult, but polishable. They talk. They negotiate. They work at it, sometimes deliberately, sometimes like pebbles that rub against each other in the same river.

For other couples, this irritation starts small and feels manageable but begins to grow. The dishwasher or the sheets or the towels become a flash point for larger issues that are more difficult or scarier to articulate. They push you both past the point of compromise.

This doesn't feel like something I can do for you. This feels like I'm neglecting myself.

Incompatibility is exhausting. It's demoralizing because it feels like all you want is to make things work, like all you need to do is "be open to change", but that place of peaceful coexistence keeps getting further and further away.

You finally learn there is nothing wrong with either of you. You are just different, and want different things.

The notion that "love conquers all" is a fallacy and is devoid of compassion. Despite monumental effort, we cannot stop being who we are, even when we have deluded ourselves into thinking we should.

THE HORROR!

The Antidote

Codependent relationships are relationships without any boundaries.

I cannot see where I end and another person begins, so we make decisions for each other, attempt to control one another's behavior and believe we are responsible for each other's emotions.

We confuse this with love.

Because our limits are not clear we don't know how to express our needs. We don't know how to say *"I don't really want to do that."* Or *"I disagree with that decision."* Or, we feel dismayed that the other person is failing to make us happy.

We feel inadequate, worthless, bitter, resentful.

And one day I realize: it's not that there is something wrong with me. It's that I have no control over another person's emotions.

It's not that I am failing. It's that I can't fix you.

It's not that I am selfish. It's that you need to rescue yourself.

So now I have two sacred assignments that will take dedication and daily practice.

The first is that I have to learn to trust myself (trust that I can be fully responsible for myself).

The second is that I have to put myself first. If I don't, I will lose myself in your needs, incapacitating my ability to care for mine (which defines our dynamic as toxic).

How do I do this? By listening to me, and by learning to set boundaries. This is really hard and takes a dedicated, consistent practice. Sometimes I will feel pretty adroit and sometimes I will feel like I have to start over.

In time, I am no longer afraid of you not needing me, of you being you without my direction or guidance.

I say no to you without believing this will result in you leaving me.

We will heal and restore all the things we once believed we would never get rid of: the shame, the self-hatred, the sense of worthlessness. The antidote is self-love.

Is It Controlling To Tell My Boyfriend What He Can Post?

If someone wants to control me, they want to exercise authority or domination over me or something that's mine. They want to keep me in check and reduce my ability to flourish.

Control comes from insecurity. If I can limit you, I can keep you. If I can dominate you, I won't lose you.

Except, control doesn't work. It takes the oxygen out of a relationship, suffocating it.

The moment you believe something belongs to you or that you need to control it, you will eventually lose it.

If you want to know if someone is trying to control you — or if what you are doing is trying to control someone else, here are some questions to ask yourself.

Do you feel heard, respected, considered? Is there snooping or spying? Are you frequently accused, or criticized, "for your own good"? Is discomfort handled through threats?

Is your relationship affecting the dynamic of other relationships, like you see your friends less because your significant other doesn't like them?

Does your significant other interpret you needing alone time as you not prioritizing the relationship?

Are your efforts to take care of yourself sabotaged?

Do you feel like someone in the relationship is constantly keeping score? Is love made conditional? Are guilt trips common? (*You would if you loved me.*)

Exercising control is very different from setting boundaries. Boundaries outline my limits. Control is an attempt to outline yours.

A boundary sounds like *"If you take photos of me, please don't post them on social media."*

Control sounds like *"I will tell you what you can and cannot post on social media."*

Finding Out Something Unexpected

If I find out something about my boyfriend that I didn't expect, the first thing I do is remind myself that people are who they are, not who I expect them to be.

Minding my own expectations — being aware of them and keeping them under observation — is really important to me because it's the place where all disappointment resides.

In other words: people do not disappoint us.
We disappoint ourselves.

Then, I do my very best to not judge people in any way for what they have done. This is mostly because I make mistakes every day, do things I should not have done, and accepting people as fallible, as flawed, as often unpredictable and surprising, makes it a bit easier for me to be more forgiving of my own questionable behavior.

Finally, I really love the concept of "letting it go" but I have long given up on being that illuminated. If I find out anything at all that someone important to me doesn't know I know, I definitely bring it up. Relationships live and die by clarity, by openness, and by honesty. *"I found out something about you that I would love to talk through, despite the fact you don't owe me an explanation".*

Afterwards, I know the person a bit better, understand him a bit better, open my eyes a bit wider. I have replaced my expectations — fantasy, fabrication, mirage — with something real. Which is to me the whole point of connection, and of love.

I replace my expectations with reality. Which is the whole point of love.

Expectations

There are two kinds of expectations.

Expectations that are fundamental and reasonable, and those that are completely unreasonable, even irrational — pretty much everything I've picked up from reading fairy tales and watching romantic comedies.

Here are some expectations that I think are fundamental and reasonable: I expect my partner to like me, to love me, to respect my boundaries, to value what I think and what I feel.

I expect him to assume responsibility for all his feelings and to articulate what they are so we can understand each other.

I expect a sense of safety, of stability in our relationship.

I do not expect him to save the day, rescue me, complete me, "only have eyes for me", or to be responsible for any of my emotions (such as cure me of loneliness, of inadequacy, make me happy, soothe my anxiety).

I do not expect to be his everything, to be his number one priority all the time, to keep nothing from me, to unfailingly understand me, to never disagree with me, to "just know what I want" because *"I shouldn't have to tell him."*

I do not expect him to be perfect, or be knighted.

A good way to know if my expectations are reasonable or not is to ask myself — do I only have eyes for him? Is he my number one priority at all times? Do I keep nothing from him? Do I always understand him? Do I agree with everything he says? Can I read his mind? Am I perfect? (No to everything.)

Do I like him? Love him? Respect his boundaries? Value his thinking? Do I assume responsibility for my feelings and my ability to communicate? Yes to everything — and when I don't, we've agreed to cut each other some slack and recognize we are flawed, but willing to practice.

What Is "Conditional" Love?

"Unconditional" means "absolute". It means *"I love you no matter what you do"*.

Unconditional love is not healthy, and it's not reasonable.

We (rightfully) demand things from those we love. Be considerate of me. Be respectful of me. Trust me, and be worthy of my trust. Follow through on what you say you are going to do.

I will not love you "no matter what" because that implies a love with no boundaries. Love without boundaries may sound romantic but look at it: it's the definition of unhealthy.

Love does not conquer all. Love is fragile and sacred and the worst thing we can do to love is assume it's unconditional.

This is how we take love for granted, and then wonder how we managed to lose the most important thing.

I Stroked My Man's Hair and He Thinks It's Creepy. Is It?

If I lovingly stroked someone's hair and they told me they found it creepy I would feel very hurt. I would ask other people if they find this creepy, seeking validation regarding what I did and why.

The truth is, it doesn't matter. It doesn't matter how many people are or are not creeped out by someone stroking their hair.

This is because each one of us has the right to our own experience, even if no one else on the planet concurs.

If I stroke someone's hair and it creeps them out, them being creeped out is real and valid and (this is key) has nothing to do with me. It has to do with them, their experience and whatever might have played a role in them interpreting hair stroking in this particular way.

If I embark on an argument on how this is not creepy, and bring in troops that don't find it creepy at all, I invalidate someone's very real and very sound opinion.

Instead, I would remind myself this is not related to me. I would say *"I am so sorry. If you find this creepy, I will not do it again. Can you give me an example of a gesture you would interpret as loving so I can do that instead?"*

It's really hard to respect someone's boundaries when I see love as something someone else interprets as a transgression. But the fact is, if it's their hair I am stroking, they get to decide.

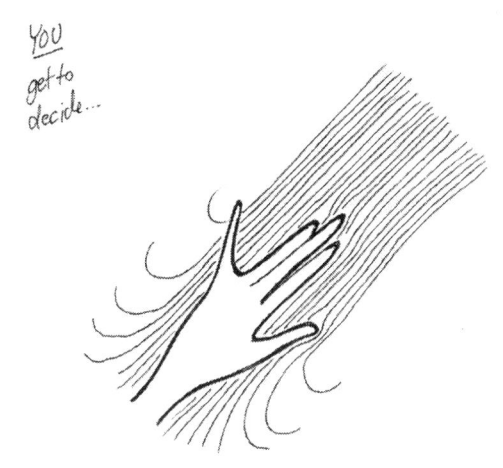

YOU get to decide...

Is It Normal if You Don't Always Want To Talk?

My significant other has a rich, complex, nuanced life. Aside from his family and friends — a multifarious cast of characters — he has a demanding job that requires a lot of his intellectual, creative and emotional energy.

On any given day, he experiences things like joy, sadness, happiness, exasperation, anger, frustration, perplexity, stress. These feelings can be manageable or can make him feel overextended. In the early evening he might feel like he needs time to process, to recover, like he doesn't feel like talking.

What this means is that there are many, many reasons he might not feel loving or affectionate that have nothing to do with me.

What it means is that, fortunately, I am not the center of the world.

Why Do Some People Not Say "I Love You"?

Because it's complicated.

Because what if this is temporary?

Because what if it doesn't work out?

Because I'm not ready.

Because I want to be sure.

Because I can't take it back.

Because I don't want to wear it out.

Because I feel it, but not all the time.

Because I don't want to expose myself like that.

Because it feels like weakness.

Because it makes me feel anxious.

Because it's not a part of my regular vocabulary.

Because I don't deserve to feel this way and I don't deserve for anyone to feel this way towards me.

Because I'd rather show you.

Is It Normal To Feel Crowded in My Relationship?

A relationship takes up a lot of time, a lot of energy and a lot of mental power. If I am not used to it, its arrival will definitely knock my life out of the pace and rhythm that I know.

In a sense, everything needs to be recalibrated.

Two things help me work through this.

The first is self-awareness. This sounds like:

I feel pressure to talk all the time. I think this pressure is coming from me rather than from you but it would help if we can together establish a pace that works for both of us.

I feel you will get angry if I tell you I need some time to myself and as a result I feel really suffocated. I realize this is coming from my assumptions and not from you.

I worry a lot about hurting your feelings when I say I can't see you every day. Can we talk early in the week about how we see the week unfolding so we can align our expectations?

The second is a combination of communication and boundaries. I clearly articulate how I feel and what I need. Here are a few examples:

I have not been in a relationship in a while (or, ever). This is all new to me and I get easily emotionally inundated. The best I can do is share these feelings with you so you know what is going on inside of me.

I am feeling a bit overloaded today. I'm going to go home early.

I really enjoyed our Saturday together. I am going to spend Sunday alone as my system feels like it's overflowing.

Be patient with yourself. Stand up for yourself. Listen to what you need, and make sure you get it.

It's quite common to feel this way and for couples to work together in an effort to find a cadence that works for both of them.

What Kind of Partner Can Guarantee a Stable Relationship?

There are no guarantees in relationships — none. Uncertainty is here to stay.

And, the surest path for me to find any kind of stability is to work on things that are inside of me.

The most destabilizing force in all my relationships is me.

Chapter 8

Secrets, Lies, Warnings, and Let-Downs

How Can I Keep a Relationship Secret?

Keeping a relationship secret means nearly every answer you give to every normal, everyday question will be a lie.

What did you do today? What's new? Where have you been?

How are you?

It means that to everyone who loves you, you will be living a double life, appearing single when you are not. Appearing alone when you are not. You will miss an assortment of meaningful events and will have no reasonable explanation. A thousand different stories you tell will not check out.

It means the person you are in this relationship with will only see one dimension of you: the one becoming an expert at deception.

This person will not meet your family. Will not meet your friends. Will not frequent the places you frequent. Will not be in the room where you get the award you've been working so hard for. Will not be with you on your birthday. Will not celebrate holidays with you. Will not be a witness to your life.

You will create a situation where you have no one to talk to. How can you talk about something that to others does not exist?

Simple things that are available to every relationship will not be available to you. A double date. Walking outside in the sun. Holding hands in public. Becoming "them" or "we".

You will develop a craving for hidden places with no light. You will collect keys that once opened hotel room doors but that now open nothing.

You will live inside a paradox: keeping a secret takes tremendous amounts of effort and work and you will have zero to show for it.

In the end, it will all come crumbling down over nothing. A photo someone posted on social media. A tiny act of carelessness — only one — in a life you have stunted with your discretion.

Only then you will realize that you spent time creating a distance between you and everything that was important to you. A distance that is hard to repair, as the only one who has words for it is you.

What if Your Boyfriend Called You by His Ex's Name?

My current partner is loving, thoughtful, generous and snuggly and makes me feel every day like I won the lottery (because, I did).

He has called me by his ex's name a handful of times and when he does he looks at me with those big beautiful eyes of his looking positively mortified, like *"I don't even know how to attempt to repair this terrible thing I have done."*

I look right at him and say, *"Don't even spend a single second worrying about it, dude."*

If someone is in our life for years and then a new person is in our life it's impossible for us not to sometimes slip.

We slip not because there is anything confusing about it, not because it means anything, but because we are human.

Being called by someone else's name is to me 100% in the (large) category of *"you know what? I'm going to let this one slide."*

Why Doesn't My Boyfriend Tell His Kids About Me?

My parents divorced when I was five years old.

Any person either of them introduced me to would to them be a significant other but to me would instantly become a parental figure.

This person would have a lasting impact on my psychology, my relationships, my ability to relate to and emotionally attach to others.

A parental figure influences my ability to draw boundaries, the way I lead my life, my self-esteem and my identity.

To me, being introduced to my significant other's children is not related to his feelings for me, his level of commitment, or his love.

It has nothing to do with me.

To me it's related to him doing what is best and healthiest for his children, and, shouldn't that be priority number one for us both, if we consider each other life-partners?

Can I Be Jealous of My Boyfriend's Dead Wife?

Anything you might feel — anything — is ok.

This is because a feeling is a feeling: unbridled, ungovernable, volatile, impetuous.

Feel your feelings. Turn them over. What are they really trying to tell you?

Maybe that you are in love, that you feel vulnerable, that you are up against something intangible, like a ghost. Maybe you feel like you can't win.

It's ok to feel anything.

What's not OK is to take a feeling and throw it around, use it to hurt someone else, demand something from someone else, control someone else. You can't turn your feelings into a weapon. You can't turn it into evidence that you have been wronged.

A feeling belongs to you, and as such it's your job to manage it.

What Happens When You Ignore Red Flags?

I sure wish there was an obvious answer to your question. Something like "you ignore + red flags = you get hurt."

This would indicate the existence of a formula. A clear path. An ironclad guarantee.

Precise steps to take to get a relationship right, and the assurance that I will not get hurt.

The term "red flag" makes it sound like the answer is vigilance. All I need to do is be on the lookout for an inkling on what awaits me.

This will grant me a sign, a "yes/no" to the question I truly want the answer for: If I give you my heart, are you going to break it? If I steer clear of every red flag, will I be safe?

Alas. You will not.

We are — all of us — a field of red flags. A landmine, human booby traps. If what you are looking for is a red flag free woman, you would not date me.

My heart has been broken by men who on paper seemed like they would never hurt me.

I have ignored enormous, flapping red flags that obstructed my view of half the sky and ended up in a relationship with a man who turned out to be caring, interesting and all out wonderful.

So, of course, pay attention. Be careful who you allow into your life. But also, know that you are never safe. Love is risky and your only protection is not in what you detect in others but in self-love.

It's loving myself that guides me into never settling for less than kind, imperfect, flawed, deep love.

What's the Best Way To Answer "Does This Make Me Look Fat?"

Once, hanging out with friends, my good friend asked her boyfriend if the dress she was wearing made her look fat.

His reaction was instant and devoid of hesitation. He got up, walked over to her and very lovingly, very gently said *"I am not doing this. This question is a trap, and you will be unhappy with any answer. I think you are beautiful, and anything beyond that is something for you to work out with yourself."*

Later that night my friend and I spoke a lot about this common dynamic and how we needed to make it a point to change the question.

If what we want is love and attention, shouldn't the question be positive rather than negative, light rather than heavy?

— um, does this shirt make my ass look awesome?

DZPR

Why Did My Boyfriend Lie About Me?

When my boyfriend says something that runs counter to how I see myself I find it so hurtful and so perplexing.

So, I defend.

"What? But, I've always ___! And, I have never ___! How can you possibly believe this to be true!? How can you be so wrong about me?"

I've learned the hard way that defending myself closes me off. It's not helpful. It does not resolve whatever we are fighting about, and often makes things worse.

So, I try to do something incredibly, agonizingly difficult. Instead of defending, I respond with curiosity.

"You believe that _____? I would love to hear more about why you feel this way."

This is more likely to lead to a conversation.

Then, I would truly listen. I would listen to what gave him this impression, and make understanding him a priority over my fury and indignation, over demanding to be perceived a certain way.

The result is that I practice paying attention. I practice taking responsibility. I learn more about how I come across. I am shown something I might be completely blind to.

I practice accepting that I am never 100% right.

All these things will improve not only my relationship to my significant other, but my relationship to everyone.

Should You Change Yourself for Someone?

When I find myself in the presence of needing to change, I ask myself if this change will force me to be someone I'm not or if it instead will make me more of who I know I can be.

These questions are not related to my feelings for another, if I love him a lot or a dash or if I just feel like I might. They are related to me.

Setting aside this specific relationship, will this make me better? Will this make me closer to the person I want to become?

If so, yes, please — change me. Erase all those things that are not really who I am anymore. Cancel them out. Make me more of all the things I'd like to be.

One of the most arresting, dazzling things about love is its cosmic, tectonic ability to transform. Even in minute amounts, love is metamorphosis, and I want all of it.

What Seemingly Small Thing Destroys Relationships?

Television.

Sitting in front of the TV is pure deception. It's disguised as something we do together, but really we watch television alone even when someone is sitting right next to us, eyes vacant, attention on a box, shushing whoever wants to say anything.

Our brains are not even on.

"Let's watch another episode" sounds like complicity but it's time away from true connection, from tell me about your day, from tell me what you are thinking, what you are feeling, tell me about the book you are reading.

It's a flickering blue light with a scene taking place somewhere else, instead of communion, you and me, here and now.

Then we wonder what happened to our relationship, how we ended up becoming so distant, how we never really had any time.

Where does it all go? We will never know.

Television is really fun. It's an escape, a mini-vacation. But, should we really allow it to be what we do every night? What happened with our walks, with snuggling, making dinner, making love?

What happened with finding each other interesting?

Besides, I can tell you now what will happen to that show you've given hours to. It will be so very good, and then not. You will force yourself to sit through unsatisfactory, poorly written seasons to find out what happens to characters that don't exist, as your significant other, real, tangible, becomes first a roommate, then a stranger.

Acting Like I Don't Care

Sometimes, I try to act like I don't care mostly because my brain tells my feelings they shouldn't feel the way they do.

As if feelings were children and my brain was the adult.

Come on, people. Keep it together. Act your age. Sit up straight. Stop it with being so irrational.

So there I am, pretending. And my feelings, instead of piping down, begin to look for louder ways to express themselves.

No one reacts well to being silenced.

My performance, not very good to begin with, begins to crack. Feelings seep out. What a mess.

Me, but miffed, indignant, silent. Me with a chip on my shoulder. Me, mumbling.

Then, passive aggressive. *"Dushka, what's wrong?"* to which I whisper *"nothing"*.

So there he is, not knowing what's happening, and here I am, pretending it doesn't matter.

We can't address what we don't articulate.

And finally I say *"I shouldn't care but I do. Here it is. It's not on you, it's on me, and I need to work it out but wanted you to know."* Or, *"I shouldn't care, but I do. When you do that, it hurts."*

This reminds me of two things. The first is my feelings deserve to be both acknowledged and respected by me. They are not children. They are trying to tell me something.

The second: Sometimes it's difficult to address something directly. But when I act I drag it on, and when I talk it's hard but then it's done.

What Is a Rookie Mistake in Your First Year of Marriage?

Humans pair up and immediately ensure their deterioration.

I am the organized one, so I will take over our social planning. You cook. I clean. Obviously you take out the garbage.

As time goes on, things I was not inclined to do become things I never do. Whatever weak muscles I had become weaker.

I atrophy in odd, indispensable places.

I fall into a deep rut that's hard to break out of, then complain my relationship lacks luster and zip.

Adventure is big but also it lives in the details I relinquish to make my day more comfortable.

I have nothing against comfort, but too much is deadly. This is how my once impassioned life goes on automatic and I begin not being present for this relationship I am increasingly dependent on.

If something doesn't come easy to me — say, remaining financially organized — I am supposed to do more of that, rather than less.

Of course it's difficult. This indicates I should be practicing, rather than abandoning the activity.

Wake up. Engage. Make an effort. Become good at what you think you are bad at.

Resist roles. Switch tasks.

Bonus: develop gratitude for all the things your significant other does that to you have become invisible.

Are Misunderstandings Normal?

Misunderstandings can be so very disheartening.

How could you? How could you not know what I meant, when we are so connected?

It's not just that misunderstandings are normal: it's that they are inevitable. We bring into every conversation our imperfect words and our inherently human communication clumsiness.

This is how what I said is not at all what I meant. This is how I read what you said in a completely different way than you intended.

This is how I can say *"I need a bit of time to myself"* and you can hear *"I don't want to be with you."*

This is how you can say *"I'm going to dinner with a friend"* and I can hear *"I'd rather spend time with my friend than with you."*

So, what can I do?

What I can do is relinquish trying to get everything perfect. You, us, your words and mine.

What I can do is accept that I will never get it right.

Perfection matters so much less than a willingness to come back, again and again, not just to the place where I try to get you to understand me, but to the place where I set myself aside to understand you.

How Do You Say I Love You Without Saying It?

I ask them about their day and then I listen.

I ask them about their life and remember. What does he worry about? What has hurt him? What is his story? What are his fondest memories? What is he working towards?

I tell the truth. This is about honesty but also about showing who I am.

I show respect. This is, to me, the opposite of taking someone for granted.

I show admiration. This is easy. He's terrific.

I compliment them. He really does look incredibly sexy with those reading glasses.

I give them my full attention. No distractions, no interruptions, no phones.

I set boundaries. Without boundaries it's impossible to nurture healthy relationships. I want to avoid coming from a place of resentment.

I accept influence. This is really hard for me — I consider making my own decisions a mark of independence. But accepting influence — the ability to share important decisions — strengthens relationships.

I say *"I love you"* at least twice a day.

Are White Lies Acceptable?

Deciding to lie to my partner based on the fact the truth would hurt them means I feel the need to manage someone else's reality. I think that's terribly presumptuous.

In addition, reality is relentless and resists distortion. It has a tendency to catch up to any lies anyone has been telling.

It's for these two reasons that I don't think lies are a good strategy.

What Are Some Examples of Criticism?

Criticism is anything I say that is directed at the person, rather than at the action.

It's the negative expression of what I want.

It's *"you always"* or *"you never"* instead of *"I wish"*.

For better results, I need to learn to say how I feel as neutrally as possible, then add the positive need.

"You never pay attention to me!" is criticism. To transform it, it might become *"I feel so lonely. I would love it if we could hang out without interruptions."*

"I can't believe you could be so uncaring!" is criticism. It might become *"When you look at your phone when we are talking, it makes me feel I'm not important to you."*

Criticism does not give me the space to review how I can improve. It makes me feel like I'm being attacked, so what I do is defend, rather than listen. It's for this reason that criticism never results in a change of behavior: this is true both when we criticize others, and when we are critical of ourselves.

Why Are Relationships Full of Doubt?

I live in a small apartment with big windows and have a number of plants.

I am trying to take care of them and wonder every morning if I am doing things right.

Are they happy where they are? Do they need more sun? Less?

Am I watering them too much? Am I not watering them enough?

Am I little by little, day by day, going to do something that will kill them?

Maybe it's true that relationships are full of doubt but I can't think of anything in life that is not.

What if He Wishes He Was Single?

When I am in a relationship, there are times when I wish I was single. When I'm employed there are times I wish I was not. When I travel to beautiful, faraway places I often wish I was home.

It's completely normal to be in a situation and wish for another.

If my boyfriend told me that sometimes he wished he was single, or if he said he was sometimes attracted to other women, or that sometimes he longs to walk away from it all, buy a motorcycle and drive down to the southernmost tip of the continent, I would nod and ask him to tell me more. I'd be quite happy to hear him fantasize out loud, as at the root of a healthy relationship is the intimacy in telling another what you secretly dream about.

To me, the question is — is this just a fantasy, a fleeting human desire to do something other than what you are doing? Or is he feeling uncertain about us? Is he being open, honest, exhibiting the emotional safety implicit in telling me everything, or is he feeling things out because he wants out of the relationship?

The only way to know is to ask.

I most definitely do not want to be with someone who is not sure about wanting me. But also, I most definitely want to be with someone who dreams, and dreams out loud, even if some of those dreams are not about me.

Is It Possible for Someone to Love You and Lie to You?

This question assumes that somehow love makes you immaculate.

It's entirely possible for someone to truly love you and hide things from you. It's possible — and extremely common — for someone to love you and lie to you.

And, yes. It's possible for someone to truly, deeply love you and cheat on you.

The assumption that somehow love arrives, blows through me and renders my behavior impeccable is a fallacy.

What someone does or doesn't do or how he behaves is not related to either my worth or his feelings for me.

YES. THIS CAN HAPPEN.

Can We Be Married but Live Separately?

Let's set marriage aside for a moment to make a bigger, more useful point.

One of the most difficult lessons to arrive at a better life is this: just because "everyone" does things a certain way, doesn't mean that way will work for me.

Just because something doesn't work for "everyone" doesn't mean it won't be perfect for me.

This imperative has been so useful to me:
Evaluate everything.

Disregard what works for others, to determine what works for me.

What works for others is nothing but noise — an impediment to really listening to myself.

Making decisions because it's what others do is the surest way to end up in the wrong life.

You can absolutely be married and live in separate places. It's your marriage. It's your life. As the only person who then has to live it, you get to decide.

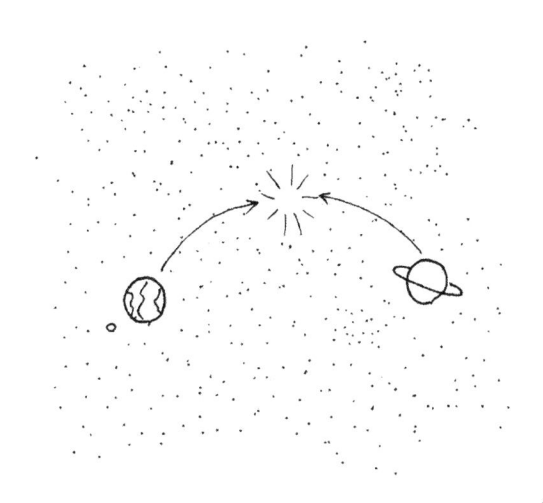

Do You Recognize When Your Partner Needs Your Help?

I don't need to be hypervigilant. I don't need to constantly guess. I don't need to risk jumping to the wrong conclusion, or risk making inaccurate assumptions, which in turn lead to me spinning stressful stories that are not real.

I can just ask.

Conversely, if I expect another person to somehow know what it is that I want, to guess what I need or how I feel, this is an unreasonable, unhealthy expectation that will lead to me disappointing myself.

We are, each one of us, responsible for articulating what we think, what we feel and what we need, which in turn increases our chances of our needs being met, and of being understood.

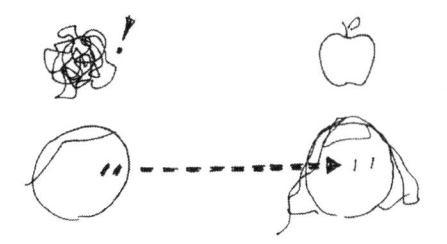

What Have You Grown To Love More About Your Partner?

There are many, many things I've grown to love more about my partner but the first one that comes to mind is the way he instantly accepts my perspective.

Let's say we're running late. We're scrambling and stressed and I will say *"Aaaah! We should have started getting ready earlier!"*

Here he could reply with *"I picked you up right on time"* or *"I suggested setting the alarm half an hour before"* or even *"hey it's not on me we're running late"* but instead he will say *"you're right! We'll do that next time!"*

I find the way he takes responsibility or acknowledges the role he played in whatever it is we are disagreeing about to be such a mark of self-confidence. I find it deeply soothing, totally disarming, and it's teaching me so much about how I don't need to be so quick to defend myself.

What I'm beginning to understand is that I can be both fallible and worth loving.

Does He Still Feel the Same Way?

I want time to stop. I want to have what we have now forever, the enthusiasm and the wonder, the discovery and effervescence.

Love is the opposite of stagnant. It's energy and flow. It moves so fast, a shape-shifter, like water. It will never be a rock.

I 100% guarantee that my significant other will soon not feel the same anymore. "Feeling the same" is not how love behaves.

Upset

When someone I love is upset, here is what I try to remember to do:

I resist the urge to "cheer her up" or change her mood. Instead I respect the place she is in and what she is feeling.

I make this about the person who is upset, not about me. This means two things: 1) I don't need to fix this or save her. 2) I need to refrain from assuming this is about me. (If it is, I will know soon enough.)

I express interest. *"I am very interested in you and how you are feeling. Can you tell me more about it?"*

I offer support. *"If you want to talk I'd love to listen; and if you are not ready to talk I'm happy to just sit with you."*

I remove any pressure. *"You don't have to do anything right away. How you feel is very important to me, and you should take your time."*

I make an offer that is open-ended. *"If there is a specific way I can support you, I'd love to hear what that might look like."*

A Few Things To Practice

Notice when you place yourself at the center of the story. This looks like any attempt to control an outcome, fixing, helping, changing. It means demanding that someone meet my needs (that's my job). It means keeping score. Placing myself at the center of things causes disconnection.

Practice getting better at listening. No interruptions. No thinking what you are going to say next. No defending. No arguing. No saving. Just listen.

Start any discussion with your feelings, rather than his behavior. If he's been working late, say *"it makes me feel like I don't matter to you"* rather than *"you are so careless with our relationship!"*

Try positive statements instead of negative statements. Instead of *"all you ever do is spend time with friends!"* try *"I would love it if we could set time aside just for the two of us."*

Point out the good, instead of the bad. Instead of asking him to change or adjust or improve, tell him all the things you appreciate about him. The more personal, the better.

Try something new. Resist the rut of always doing the same things, even if it feels comfortable and familiar, and try new things (go on a hike you've never been on!). Extra points if you learn something new together (learn a new language, then plan a trip where that language is spoken).

I Wish I Could Change

Over the years if there ever was friction in my relationships, the way I processed it was: I wish I could change. I wish I could change to accommodate this.

I didn't really ever think *"I wish he could change"*.

My work has been on accepting — and loving — who I am, in understanding that incompatibility means *"we are different, and that is OK"* rather than *"clearly there is something wrong with me"* or *"one of us is in the wrong."*

Here is where I think the magic happens: when I fully accept who I am, and fully accept who he is, and we both change, evolve, not as a result of wishing or accommodating or pleasing or compromising or controlling, but as a result of becoming better for being together.

Fight To Grow Closer

When you fight, do you look to prove the other wrong? To take the other person down? Are you deliberately hurtful? Insulting? Exposing? Do you alter what took place?

What happens to you when you fight? Does it feel like a catastrophe you will not survive? Does your heart race? Can you think straight? Can you communicate clearly? Are you passive-aggressive? Do you cease to engage, walk away?

When you fight do you beat yourself up? *Why can't I ever learn? Why is this happening again?*

When you fight, do you put any thought into what the fight is about, or do you believe the small issue is the real problem?

Fighting fair means self-awareness. It means fighting to understand, rather than fighting to win. It means listening, putting yourself in the other person's place; expressing yourself clearly and respectfully.

It means taking action if something bothered you instead of pushing the incident aside.

It means doing the opposite of "never go to bed angry". If you feel exhausted, like you are jumping out of your skin, like you can't stop crying, like you are going to say something you will regret, you take a break.

Fighting fair means self-compassion. What do you need? A time out, a glass of water, a moment to tell yourself you are doing the best you can, instead of raging at yourself?

Fighting fair means relinquishing the need to control and trusting that you both want the same thing.

It means thinking about what you want to say and turning it into an "I feel" sentence, instead of a "you" sentence. (*"I feel like I don't matter"*, rather than *"you are so inconsiderate!"*)

Fighting fair means feeling safe even when you are fighting, and making sure the person you are fighting with feels safe too.

AND THE WINNER IS...!

What Is the Biggest Failure in Modern Marriage?

In the beginning, marriage had nothing to do with love. Rather than the luxury we now nonchalantly refer to as "emotional connection," marriage was a practical matter, about survival, protection and shelter.

As it evolved, marriage became about security, property rights, bloodlines and alliances between families. In matters of marriage, women were regarded as things — property.

Men became by law husbands of their dead brother's widow.

It wasn't until later that marriage began to consider the importance of the couple's consent.

The notion of associating marriage with romance, love and companionship is still new, and neither pervasive nor prevalent.

Depending on where you are, marriage now might be considered something closer to a bond, about commitment and responsibility.

In some countries couples today consider marriage something related to discovery, growth, exploration. What is this thing called life? Can we figure it out together?

More people are getting divorced than ever, but this points more towards autonomy, respect and independence than it does to the crumbling of an institution that must evolve to remain relevant.

Institutions are created to make our lives better. We don't serve them. They serve us.

We expect more from marriage today — a consensual partnership rather than a life sentence.

Modern marriage is just beginning to regard its participants as human, as equipped with emotions, as equals, instead of as a transaction. This is an improvement.

There is no failure in modern marriage.

MARRIAGE   ALSO MARRIAGE

DZDR

Chapter 9

Letting Go

What Do I Do if He Drains Me but I Love Him?

Step one: spend some time alone. You need the silence to hear yourself.

Step two: ask yourself. What is it about the relationship that is draining?

Step three: write out boundaries that protect all of you. Him, you, your energy, your relationship.

Here are some examples of what that might look like:

We are spending a lot of time together and I need a day, a week all to myself.

I would like some quiet time in the evenings. This is so I can wind down and get a good night's sleep.

Sometimes, when we talk, I need time to think about things. I won't always have an answer right away.

You are very important to me but some decisions I make are about my life and as such I have to make them on my own.

Step four: talk to him about your boundaries. Be gentle, but firm. Be good about enforcing them, even if it means feeling like he is pushing, even if it feels uncomfortable.

Step five: recognize your boundaries are fluid, not static. *I would love to spend a quiet Sunday with you.*

Will Lack of Attention End a Relationship?

Attention is everything.

Attention is the foundation of every relationship. It's my daily work. It's showing interest in the person that you love, listening, asking questions. It's putting your phone down, defying a life full of distractions that expertly disguise themselves as important and urgent.

It's from the attention you grant me that I deduce I matter to you, that I learn to trust you, that I create a bond, an emotional connection. It's how I determine I can count on you.

It's attention that creates resilience.

When we fight, the fight will rock us and the structure we have built. If we have a history of paying attention we recover from fights because our foundation is solid.

Over time, a lack of attention ends a relationship because in the most fundamental way I have not been present for it: we've got an assortment of building blocks of different colors and sizes, without the glue.

Is Arguing a Sign of Passion?

Love is not conflict. Love is not drama. Love is not combat. Love is not struggle.

Arguing is not a sign of passion. Arguing is a sign of disagreement.

It's an indication that you believe one thing and I believe another. Arguing is how we show each other why we believe what we believe.

If I instead believe that arguing is a sign of passion, then arguing becomes not something I want to resolve but something I want to provoke. Something I seek. Something I want.

It means I feel there is something wrong with us when we are not arguing.

It means that when we don't argue, I feel unloved.

It's a trap. Don't fall for it.

Do You Have a Moral Obligation To Stay in Your Relationship?

If I remain in a relationship because of a moral obligation, I give the person I am with no choice but to spend their life in a loveless relationship because of my sense of duty.

I fail to see the morality of this arrangement.

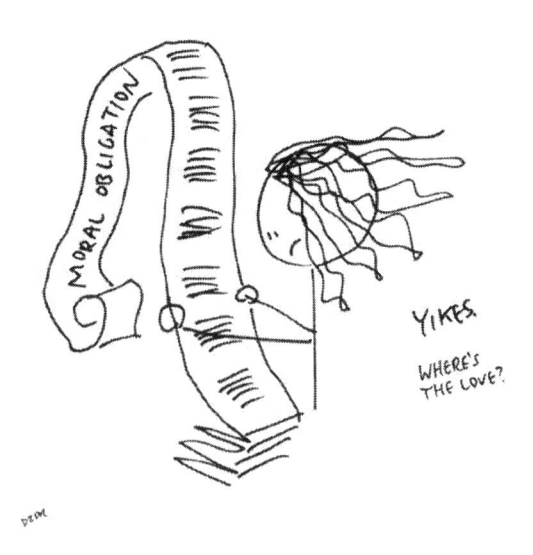

We Have Everything

In the beginning all we did was enthusiastically engage in wanton, excessively luxurious sex.

We'd have sex and talk, alternating between these two excellent activities, whittle away hours, afternoons, weekends, making love and talking.

What did we talk about? I don't know. The slope of your back. The curve in my hip. We'd rewrite the past to better prove the existence of a miracle in our love story. *"I knew right from the beginning"* he'd say. He'd tighten his arm around my waist. *"Kiss me."*

We worried so much about all the things we were not getting done, the time we were frittering away.

"Wow," he'd say, both concerned and astonished. *"All we do is have sex."*

"Someday," we'd say. *"Someday we'll get our act together."*

Was it reckless? Were we careless? I don't know.

As time went by, things got better, I suppose. We got organized, learned to prioritize, checked things off our to-do list, felt productive. Our lives, efficient, ran like clockwork, every minute put to good use. How buttoned up. How adult of us.

Except we'd wake up feeling distant, listless, maybe even trapped in a life of our own creation. Our schedule, demanding, relentless, self-inflicted.

Can you remind me where it was we wanted to go?

"Remember the early days?" we'd say, wistful, nostalgic. *"Remember the early days when all we managed to do was waste time?"*

We spend our whole lives anxious, fretting, wishing for who knows what, neglecting to notice that it's right now that we already have everything.

How Do I Become "Good Company"? My Boyfriend Says I'm Not.

Some day, hopefully not too far into the future, a series of huge realizations will click for you, as follows:

My god. My boyfriend's opinion of me does not define me. What he says and thinks is not the measure of my worth. It is unrelated to me and related instead to him. It's not that I'm not good company — it's that he's cruel to people who love him.

Wait a minute. I am actually quite lovely and what I need to do is start expressing my preferences and my opinions instead of attempting to accommodate what other people say they want me to be.

Oh, wow. I don't need to be "more fun". What I need is family, friends and a lover who believes what I have finally understood: That I'm already engaging and if anyone doesn't think so then they are not for me.

I'm not for everybody, and this is an excellent thing.

And, you know what? I am at my wit's end with people who have an important place in my life and put me down. We all deserve better than someone who belittles us and as such I need to review who I allow into my life.

Before all these things click for you, you will feel so stuck. You will feel bereft, wondering what you are missing, what it is you need to change to finally be loved in the way that you wish you could be loved.

And I am here to just hand you the answer: nothing. You need to change nothing, other than set boundaries and say goodbye to anyone who does not treat you like something precious and valuable and worthy of respect.

For now, you will not believe me, but my hope is that someday you will.

Stonewalling

Stonewalling is the act of shutting down. In the middle of an argument I stop engaging and build a wall, encasing myself in it. I become unresponsive, tune out, turn away, put my head down, leave the room.

If I am stonewalling you, attempting to communicate with me is exasperating, frustrating, heartbreaking, because I have checked out.

I have emotionally abandoned you.

Stonewalling has been identified as one of the four most destructive behaviors in a relationship.

Do you know who does this awful thing? Me. In bad fights I withdraw and become impossible to reach and it's because I cannot. Fight. Anymore. I feel utterly overwhelmed. The psychological term is "flooded".

I have gotten a lot better at this because I learned a very simple thing: that I can ask for a break.

"I am so sorry. I have reached my limit. I need to take this up later, or tomorrow."

I had always been told not to go to bed angry and I want to get relationships right so I didn't know I could do this. Giving myself permission to ask for a time out has been life-altering. It is the single most important thing I have learned to fight better. I feel relieved just telling you about it.

Now that we've gotten stonewalling out of the way, I will add that there is another behavior that is even worse: worse in that it shows to be the single predictor of the end of a relationship. It's called "contempt."

Contempt is treating another person without respect. It's being condescending, hostile, mocking. It's eye rolling. It's raising your voice, yelling at someone. It's attacking another person's sense of self.

If anyone raises their voice at me, it shatters something inside of me. I find it so diminishing, so aggressive and painful, that I cannot allow it. I protect myself by leaving, not just the room but the relationship.

If you want to read more about these behaviors (and their antidotes), I recommend anything written or developed by The Gottman Institute. Look up "The Four Horsemen/The Gottman Institute."

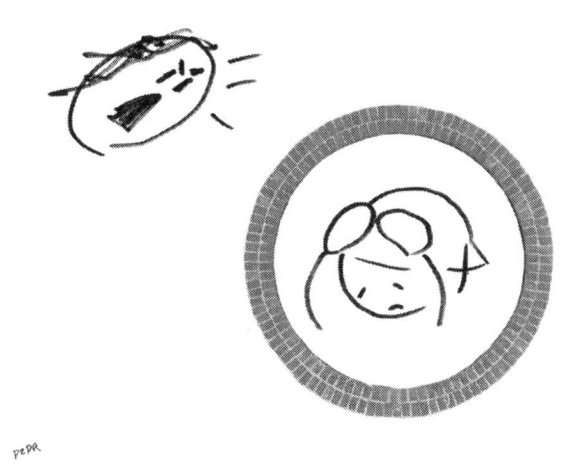

Can We Avoid Conflict for a Healthy Relationship?

A healthy relationship is not one devoid of conflict. That would be an impossible expectation. Relationships don't demand impossible things from us. They are reasonable, a skill, and we can learn and get better.

We experience conflict because we are human. We feel frustrated, irritated, slighted, tired, triggered, angry, ruffled, upset. We raise our voices, say things that are critical, walk away.

We hurt the people that we love.

We fight, often about the same things.

It's what we do after we fight that determines the health of a relationship. Healthy couples figure out how to repair the damage they have caused after the fight.

It's this — repair — not the absence of conflict, that makes relationships strong, resilient.

We can't avoid conflict but we can learn how to fight, learn how to come back from a fight with the right tools to repair our relationship.

In repairing, we learn we are steady, we are strong, and we are safe. Repair says *"you may not be perfect, but you are so worth the work."* It says *"this may be hard, but I'm not going anywhere."*

Stop

I want to stop time.

I want to stop it when I'm laughing and I want to stop it when I'm tasting something delicious and I want to stop it when my nephew, disheveled hair and big beautiful eyes, is patiently explaining something to me.

I want to stop time when I'm with you.

It's this fervent desire to stop time — *please, please, please just freeze this frame it's happening too fast I can't remember what it was like to kiss you* — that contributes to me missing the very moment I want to preserve.

What Are Some Things You Wanted To Say but Didn't?

I'm enchanted by the noises he makes when he's deeply involved in any everyday thing, like drinking water. The slurp, the grunt, the moan, the sigh. It's like having a wild animal over for a visit.

"Someday," he says *"what you find so endearing will irritate the crap out of you."*

But, why? Why can't you always look at me like that? Why can't we always hug long and tight and urgent under the frame of the entrance door? Why can't I always interpret your arrival as a miracle instead of part and parcel of the stream of people life typically brings?

Except, I know.

I know impermanence wins.

And that's why I can't say anything.

Why Is It Hard To Leave Someone Who Hurts You?

Have you ever heard of the term "trauma bond"?

When we go through something difficult (as children) and don't ever look at it, recognize it, work on it or resolve it, we look to replicate it in our adult relationships.

We want to act it out, repeat it over and over, in an attempt to address it, but also because this is what we know. This is called a trauma bond.

What we learn as kids is to turn our back on ourselves in exchange for getting the love we crave. The same methodology we established with our caregivers is the one we will in the future recognize as familiar.

When I say "trauma" I mean any event where I felt I had no agency. If when I was a kid I lived in a state of chaos, if I felt I needed to leave my needs unexpressed to, say, keep the peace, then that's what I will look for: relationships that feel chaotic where I never express my needs.

A trauma bond as an adult feels extremely intense, like an obsession. (*I can't get enough of you, and I cannot leave you.*) It expresses itself in an absence of boundaries. (*I don't ever say no to you.*)

If I am in any way hurting myself to keep your attention I cannot recognize it — or, I see exactly what is happening (*oh, whoa, this is a trauma bond!*) but feel powerless to do anything about it.

It is extremely painful.

To heal this kind of dynamic, we need to put ourselves first, starting right now. We need to draw boundaries and state our needs as clearly as possible. As we do this again and again our relationships change: we understand our worth and begin to find people who are supportive, rather than feeling like everyone around us is taking advantage of us.

This is why learning how to love ourselves is so critical to happiness.

We've all been hurt. We are all scared of being abandoned. We all feel somehow inadequate. We are all hungry to be seen.

This is why it's so important to grant others our full attention.

They, like us, have spent their whole lives carrying the inevitable wounds inflicted on us when we were children.

I've Never Opened the Door for Her and Now She's Angry. What Do I Do?

Fights are seldom about what they appear to be about.

They are really about my garbled interpretation of your behavior.

"I'm hurt you didn't return my call" is not about the call. If I paused and really thought about it I would say *"I'm scared I don't matter to you anymore."*

"You are working all the time" becomes *"I don't occupy an important place in your life."*

When another fights over something that seems irrational, it's time to pause. *"I would love to open the door for you if that's important to you. But also, I want to listen.*

Over the past year, I have not opened the door for you, and it has never come up. So, could we please talk about what this might really be about?"

Some things are so hard to say. *"I'm feeling vulnerable." "I want more attention." "Things are kind of shaky."*

When a fight feels erratic, nonsensical, it helps a lot to assume the real reason behind it is crouching below the surface, hiding behind our insecurities.

We are all just afraid.

FIGHTS ARE NOT ABOUT WHAT YOU THINK THEY ARE ABOUT.

Chapter 10

Keeping It Going

What Are Some Ways Your Significant Other Makes You Smile?

I've noticed in many relationships a tendency to focus on shortcomings — a natural inclination towards criticism, often about petty things.

As if pointing them out has ever resulted in changing someone's behavior.

A collection of critical comments over time, no matter how small, would leave me feeling frustrated and critical of myself — a nagging sense that I simply couldn't get anything right.

My partner does the opposite. He calls out things he likes, things he enjoys, things that went well, even when they're small (*I love that dress on you! Dinner was so fun. Didn't we have a great trip? I'm proud of how we handled that. I am so lucky to have you.*) His individual comments make me smile, but I've realized it's much more significant than that.

I've noticed over time a sense of peace arises in me, one that comes from feeling appreciated rather than feeling like I keep coming up short.

It's so incredibly powerful to take the time to notice and mention what you value about someone else. This practice is like a balm. Comment by comment, notch by notch, we determine the fate of our relationships.

So Lucky

I tell my guy every day that I wonder how I got so lucky.

I could have missed this, not called him, not found him, not taken him into consideration. I could have been distracted, unreceptive, or with someone else.

He could have been busy, or in another relationship, or in another country. He could have been tied down, tied up, oblivious, otherwise engaged.

We could have been living in different times.

The fact that we were both where we were in the state that we were at the same time, the fact that we were both paying attention and recognized in each other something worth noting, makes me feel fortunate, and like life is full of serendipity and wonder.

The Most Beautiful Person Ever

I experience beauty in two ways.

The first is through my eyes. It is related to harmony, to design, to balance, to grace, to symmetry, to surprise. I find this kind of beauty extremely attractive. It makes me feel happy.

The second is through my heart. It's filled with light and feels like I can see beyond what my eyes can — a glimpse into something majestic and sacred. It's dazzling. It takes my breath away. It makes me feel a kind of faith, like I already have everything, everything. It's so intense it's often painful, like something is piercing the center of my chest.

When I feel the second kind of beauty, I blurt out *"you are the most beautiful thing I've ever seen."* And, I sure hope he believes it, because truer words have never been spoken.

Is It Realistic To Believe Love Will Last Forever?

"You are my most important thing," he whispers.

His whispers are his specialty.

"You are my most important thing, except one day you won't be."

He squeezes his eyes shut. *"I am sorry,"* he says. *"I did not need to say that and now I feel I've hurt you."*

Except, I'm not hurt. I already know feelings are perishable.

I already know that even as I write this everything will change.

He will change, and I will. Our lives, our unnatural circumstances, our dynamics, our preferences, our looks, our friends, the weather.

Beyond local meteorological conditions there will be interplanetary shifts in this and neighboring galaxies.

Asteroids will threaten our existence.

I don't embark on something because I believe in "forever".

I embark on things because I believe they are worthwhile, and because of the faith I have in my own heart's resilience.

How Do I Make My Boyfriend Believe That I Love Him?

Way before you came along, your boyfriend was being designed and brought into existence. Many elements went into his fortunate construction, resulting in the specimen you see today.

The way the hair on the side of his head does that little flip. The delicate crow's feet fanned out from his big eyes. The masterpiece color of his irises in shades of gray and green, the inner rim flecked with hazel.

The subtle shrug of his shoulders and the way he buttons up his shirt sleeves, right up to the tops of his wrists.

He was loved or not. Wounded or not. Cut open or not. Cherished, or left to die on the side of some back road. He learned his very personal, very subjective interpretation of life lessons.

The man you see before you today is evidence of whatever he had to do to survive.

It's so important to understand we have no power — and no responsibility — over the emotions of others. We cannot make someone love us. We cannot get someone to trust us. We do not have the ability to make someone happy.

You cannot fix him.

If you tell him you love him and he does not believe you, this has nothing to do with you. That compound fracture was already there the day you first met. It was already there, behind the red rimmed glasses and gentle disposition.

We all have internal work to do to scramble up to the ruthless challenge that love presents to us. In a sense, we have to break ourselves down and reassemble ourselves. We have to go out on a limb.

We have to have faith in things that maybe long ago someone proved did not merit our faith.

This is terror-inducing, and no one can do it for us.

So here is what you can do. You can work on yourself. You can peel away your own protective coating, expose yourself, challenge your own patterns, review your own subjective interpretation of life lessons.

You can take notice of the sobering fact that being loved is the very opposite of being in survival mode.

You can be a witness to his denuding and his courage. You can provide a steady counterpoint to his generous exhibitions and to the series of acts of the most intimate kind of heroism.

And, if you get really lucky, you can confirm the astonishing, often overwhelming transformative power of love.

Not because we can ever change another, but because it jolts us — like a large bucket of ice water dumped over our head — into changing ourselves.

What Is the Sweetest Thing You Can Say to Someone You Love?

I believe in you.

I am here for you.

I am not going anywhere.

I feel safe with you.

I want to listen.

Thank you.

You are right.

I see your perspective.

I completely understand.

Of course I remember.

I believe you.

I am sorry.

I feel the same way.

I love your company.

Everyday things feel special because I do them with you.

Why Are Snuggles Important?

Snuggling is magic. It's someone else and you, intertwinkled.

Snuggling is subtle and nuanced and not necessarily related to sexual contact. It can be deeply grounding, even healing.

Days are movement and bustle. They are busy, tangled, filled with friction and small disappointments. You come together irritated, miffed, ruffled, grated, sometimes even wounded.

A snuggle is a pause, a space, a bid, an offering, an opening. Here. Let the dust settle here. Breathe here. Land here.

It's a wordless let's get on the same page. It's reconciliation. It's me, arriving, feeling the safe harbor of your arms, the familiar scent of your neck.

Snuggling has the same effect as looking up at the stars: you take a deep breath. Then, gently and with wonder, it floods you with inevitable perspective.

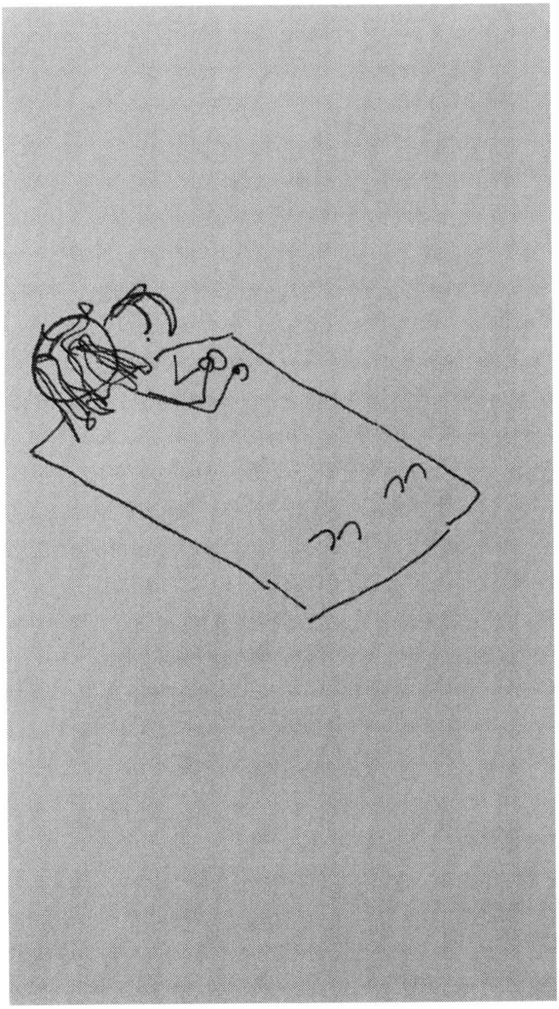

What if You Love Him but He Doesn't Make You Happy?

This is a trick question and if I don't identify it as such it will destroy me.

Being with someone I love is nothing short of a miracle. It's one of life's greatest gifts.

This question tricks me into attributing my unhappiness to the person that I love, but have I really explored why I am not happy? Can happiness really be found somewhere outside of me? Are the people we are with truly responsible for our emotional state?

What are the long term consequences of associating blame to the wrong things?

What I would do is hold on tight to the person I love and figure myself out before I go sacrificing the most valuable, least replaceable gift I have been given.

Why Do People Stay in Relationships They Know Aren't Working?

Relationships are not like rocks, inert, static, still. They are like water, in a state of perpetual motion, not necessarily in a stage of tumult but certainly in constant flux.

I can be fulfilled then not, close to you then not, feel like it's working then not, only to experience things getting increasingly better and deeper, or increasingly worse.

There are points in the relationship where I can't really make a diagnosis. Is this a rough patch, or is this not working? If we get through this, will we get stronger, or is this just a sign that things are slowly falling apart?

The members of that relationship are also like water, in their own inner state of perpetual motion and flux. Is what I am thinking and feeling happening in the relationship, or is it happening in me?

People stay in relationships they know are not working for many reasons, but one of them is because *"we are having a tough time now"* and *"this is not working"* can look very similar.

Because, *"this relationship is oppressive"* and *"the relationship is fine but I am restless"* can look very similar.

Love is a feeling and feelings can be mercurial. It helps me to ask myself — underneath that love, are we friends? Underneath that love are we building something? In the future we imagine, are we both there?

Absence of Attunement

My unhappiness in relationships invariably stems from an almost imperceptible absence of attunement.

I want togetherness, and you are somewhere else.

How can we be so out of rhythm, when we used to dance so naturally? How can I suddenly feel so deeply isolated?

Where are you, and why did you leave me here?

This experience is all a flash, an instant. But, here I am, left with this indelible stain. Disappointment.

I can't tell. Is this about what I expect, and therefore unrelated to you?

Am I reacting to your absence or to my anxiety?

We don't know why we are unhappy. We don't even know if it comes from you, or if it comes from me, or if it comes from us.

The antidote to unhappiness is exploration. You of you. Me of me. Us, exploring the relationship together.

The gigantic trap is that we have to be willing to put in the work, and the effort, and the time, which is difficult to do when what you cannot wash off is the sensation that someone has failed you.

How Can Lovers Become Strangers?

Change is inexorable. It is ever-present, within us and around us. Impermanence is the only thing we can ever be certain of.

We think change is huge, tectonic, but instead it's tiny and exists in small things. If you want to completely change your life, pick up a habit and do it over and over. It will add up to a complete transformation and astonish you with its totality.

This holds true in the reverse. Lovers become strangers to each other because their love is contained in the smallest things. We, believing it's in the big things, feel the small things are not important and stop paying attention.

This lack of attention, this turning away instead of turning towards, becomes a habit you do over and over and before you know it has added up to a complete transformation, astonishing in its totality.

You began holding tight on a raft built for two and now you are on different cruise liners that have lost sight of each other.

Why Do Passionate Relationships End?

It's not that passionate relationships end. It's that relationships go through stages. It takes love and patience and skill to navigate these stages — to appreciate each stage for what it offers, instead of wanting things to be the way they used to be.

A passionate relationship is intense and exciting. Everything is resplendent. You are. They are. The whole world is. How are you so perfect?

Life begins to get in the way. There is conflict, and experiences reveal the inevitable. Oh no. "Perfect" was an illusion. What if you leave me? What if I lose what I had before you showed up?

Do we stand there paralyzed, craving what we had? Or do we resolve to open our eyes? Can I idealize you less, see you more?

Then comes what I can only call grief. You anger me. You disappoint me. You trigger me. I want to leave. I miss being single. I miss my independence.

Do we look back and label the initial passion a lie? Or do we hold on, determined, trusting that we have found something worth sticking it out for?

So we make space. We make space for who we are, rather than what we glorified. We learn. Less control, more forgiveness. Less fantasy. More allowing ourselves to see each other for who we really are. More acceptance.

What do we find, as we go through all of this complexity? That we love each other, not what we project on the other. That we are curious. That you are an adventure, that you are wonder, and that I can predict what you will do, which is the essence of a healthy relationship.

This is the rise of a new kind of passion, one devoid of fear, that feels more like growth and less like chaos. This feels safe. This feels like home.

How Do I Get an Introvert To Talk More?

When I am going through something difficult (and sometimes not so difficult) I need time to myself. I need to grant my system a chance to process whatever is happening, and to grant my brain time to think.

I once dated a man who expressed frustration at my inability to share things with him. I tried to — I really did. But talking things through instead of letting them filter inside of me first felt like trying to think in a noisy room with loud, bad music.

I couldn't do it.

What this meant to me was that part of my personality was that of an introvert — the need to go within to untangle things. To him, this was a symptom of an absence of commitment. *"We are not deciding things together,"* he would say. *"You are deciding them on your own."*

It hurts me to think that who I am caused him pain.

In the end the conclusion I came to was that there was a woman out there who needed him, and that they would be happy sipping coffee, thinking through things together.

And that one day I'd find a guy who wouldn't mind eating breakfast in silence while I gathered all the words I was looking for to express what I wanted to say.

How Do You Know if Someone Is Your Soulmate?

I meet someone and I really like him. I am overjoyed to learn he likes me too.

We spend time together and discover many things about ourselves and each other.

We respect each other, are honest with each other, share things that often feel scary and exposing, and are willing to have every difficult conversation that presents itself.

We commit to keep coming back, to assume the best in each other, and to forgive both ourselves and each other for the many mistakes we will make.

We together navigate the changing seasons of every relationship — rather than expecting perpetual passion we value trust, reliability, sturdiness, solidity.

Together we grow, and become better people.

One day, we look back on our relationship and at how far we've come, as individuals and as a team.

And that's how I know he's my soulmate.

HOW FAR WE'VE COME.

What Does a Secure Relationship Look Like?

A secure relationship has a lot of clear, expressed boundaries in every realm: physical, emotional, sexual, material.

A secure relationship is marked by consent.

There is trust, and it's pervasive.

You assume the best in one another.

Conversations are respectful, honest and open.

You can always take a break: from a difficult conversation, from an argument, from a fight. *Can we pause and start again tomorrow?*

Messing up does not feel like your relationship is brought into question — it feels like something to work through.

People say *"I was wrong"*, *"I am sorry"* and *"I believe you."*

The relationship is free from manipulation (no guilt trips, no blame, no silent treatment, no passive-aggressive behavior) and free from retaliation.

Decisions feel balanced, a collaboration.

Life feels like a team sport.

What you share in moments of intimacy is safeguarded in a gentle place wrapped in tissue paper and never used against you.

When you share how you feel, you are understood, never invalidated, dismissed or belittled.

Your beliefs and opinions count as important even if the other person does not believe or opine in the same way.

You are never pressured, forced or controlled.

You feel heard.

You have space and privacy.

You have a life outside of the relationship, with interests and activities that matter to you, that grant you a sense of purpose.

You feel loved not for how you behave, not for what you do, but for who you are.

If "Happily Ever After" Is a Lie, What Is the Truth?

In movies and fairy tales "Happily ever after" is riding off into the sunset. It's fade to black. It's exit left. It's taking for granted that everything will be effortless and perfect somewhere out there.

In real life, one day turns into the next day. The next day, you still have to deal with you.

It's not so much that happily ever after is a lie. It's that in life, you are left holding your story.

The truth about lifelong relationships is that everything changes. You change. The person you love changes. Things that you found endearing become irritating. You are attracted to other people. You lose track of who you are. You realize you don't want what you thought you wanted.

When lifelong relationships work, they work for different reasons, but the main one, I think, is to accept that the other person is flawed. To commit to something beyond the two of you.

The truth of a lifelong relationship is accepting that sometimes you will not be happy.

THE
END.

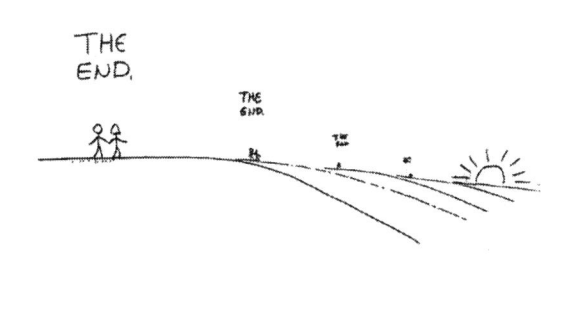

Small Gestures

Strong relationships are created by small gestures that add up. You kiss in the morning. You check in during the day. You ask just the right question — how did that important meeting go? Did your headache clear up? — you text at night before you fall asleep. It's intimate, and it builds intimacy. It's a touch. I don't want to close off my day without saying goodnight.

Like all small actions, these gestures accumulate into a relationship that becomes caring, connected, close.

The things we want — to feel seen, understood, the sense someone cares — are not in sweeping, dramatic actions or big decisions. They are not in promises or vows or declarations. They are in the smallest things.

It's hard and counterintuitive to figure out, I think: that the small things are the big things.

Meant To Be

There is no "meant to be". Counting on "meant to be" for the survival of my relationship is like navigating a ship with no rudder.

While we are at it:

Playing hard to get will attract the wrong people.

There is more than one person out there who can be wonderful for me.

True love is not necessarily synonymous with roller coasters, fireworks or sparks. Sometimes true love is steady and grows deeper with time. I don't know why we want the fairy tale when what we have is real.

The better my relationship is with myself the stronger my relationships will be. Other people do not complete me — I am already whole.

There are no soulmates, no "other half" and no "happily ever after". This is not a put down on relationships: they are to me the meaning of life. But they take hard work, and they demand that I keep showing up.

My significant other, regardless of the depth of his love, cannot read my mind. The assumption that he can somehow guess why I am hurt is not effective.

No matter how happy I am, one person can't give me everything I need. No matter how rich a relationship is, we need family and friends, interests and occupations, who all contribute to a polychromatic life.

No matter how deep and true my love is, it's common and healthy to feel attracted to other people.

Happy couples fight. Fights are necessary for growth and a lot of what makes a couple elastic is in proving to each other the relationship is resilient.

"Never go to bed angry" is nonsensical. Taking time and space and coming back to the fight with perspective is much more helpful than fighting until we are both exhausted.

If I am waiting for specific demonstrations of love, it helps to keep in mind people don't love me the way I want them to. People love me the way they know how.

Cheating has nothing to do with love. If someone cheats, it doesn't mean they don't love. It doesn't mean the relationship was not good. It means they cheated.

External forms of commitment will not make my relationship stronger. If my relationship is crumbling, getting married, buying a house, having children is not going to save us. It's like being on a sinking ship and securing a rope around my neck.

My feelings will change. They will change from day to day, from month to month, from year to year. This is why every relationship needs commitment underpinning the love.

Signs Your Relationship Will Last

We follow through on what we say we're going to do.

"We need to talk" is something we look forward to rather than dread.

We fight well and work at not leaving each other in a painful place.

We like each other.

We trust each other.

We assume the best in each other.

We want the same things.

The things that matter to me matter to him.

We practice boundaries.

We don't expect the other to "be our everything."

We spend time apart.

We work on ourselves.

We take responsibility rather than blame.

We laugh.

Why Do You Think Most Relationships Fail?

When I end a relationship one of the many feelings I contend with is that I failed. That I cannot get relationships right.

But the truth is most relationships end.

So, what is the criteria to determine if a relationship was a failure or a success?

Is the longevity of the relationship the only real measure of success? If so, what about all the people who have been in long term relationships that are so unhappy all they have accomplished is how to barely tolerate each other?

What about relationships where all parties are unhappy, distant, cruel, feel alone?

What about people who left unhealthy relationships and learned how to better love themselves, bet on themselves, believe life could be better, because there has to be something other than spending my life like this?

To me, successful relationships have very little to do with how long they lasted. Did we grow? Did we evolve? Did we learn? Did we become better people?

With this criteria, I believe most relationships succeed.

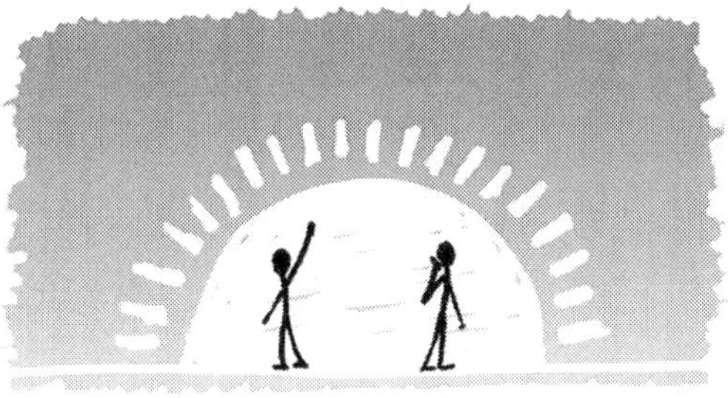

Author's note

Thank you for reading my book!

If you have questions about anything along the way, I suggest you enter my name and any key word — self-love, boundaries, communication, relationships, breaking up — in the Quora search window. This way you can find everything I've written about what you seek, and maybe come across other helpful things along the way.

You can also post comments, questions, drawings, notes, or photographs on Instagram, using the hashtag #dushkazapatapleasedontblamelove.

Also, here are other books I've written expand on what I write about here. I particularly recommend my book about boundaries *"How To Draw Your Boundaries and why no one else can help you"*, my workbook about learning how to love yourself *"The Love of Your Life is You: A Step-by-Step Workbook to Loving Yourself"* and *"Love Yourself and other insurgent acts that recast everything"*.

Remember that everything I write — including all of the content of the books I mention above — is available on Quora for free.

If you find any of this helpful, please write Amazon reviews so that other people who need it can find it too.

Dushka Zapata

San Francisco, California

December, 2022

About the Author

Dushka Zapata has worked in communications for over twenty years, running agencies (such as Edelman and Ogilvy) and working with companies to develop their corporate strategy.

During this time she specialized in executive equity and media and presentation training. She helped people communicate better through key message refinement and consistency and coached them to smoothly manage difficult interviews with press during times of crisis.

Dushka is an executive coach and public speaker who imparts workshops about personal brand development. She has been hired for strategic alignment hiring, to coach and mentor high potential individuals, improve upon new business pitches, refine existing processes and galvanize a company's communication efforts.

She recently built and ran the communications team at Zendesk then became head of communications for Forte, a start up that believes games can unlock new economic opportunities for billions of people.

She is currently head of team engagement at Forte, ensuring employees of a distributed, decentralized workplace feel connected to the organization they work for.

Dushka was named one of the top 25 innovators in her industry by The Holmes Report and regularly contributes to Quora, the question and answer site, where she has over 205 million views.

About the Illustrator

Dan Roam is the author of six international bestselling books on visual storytelling. **The Back of the Napkin** was named by Fast Company, The London Times, and BusinessWeek as the "Creativity Book of the Year".

Dan is a creative director, author, painter, and model-builder. His purpose in life is to make complex things clear by drawing them and to help others do the same. Dan has helped leaders at Allbirds, Google, Microsoft, Boeing, Gap, IBM, the US Navy, and the Obama White House solve complex problems with simple pictures.

Dan and his whiteboard have appeared on CNN, MSNBC, ABC, CBS, Fox, and NPR.

Made in the USA
Middletown, DE
21 December 2022